The Purpose of a Universe

Gam Zokanti

Mazo Publishers

The Purpose of a Universe

Gam Zokanti
perckay-GamZ@yahoo.com

ISBN 978-1-971155-01-2

Mazo Publishers
Website: www.mazopublishers.com
Email: mazopublishers@gmail.com

You may be right, I may be crazy,
But it just may be a lunatic you're looking for.

– Billy Joel

TABLE OF CONTENTS

Introduction 7

Trying To Know God 9

A Glimpse Into Heaven 10

Actual Dimensions 15

Dimensions And Reality 19

Validity And Reliability 25

Where Evidence Starts To Point 29

Significance Of Higher Dimensions 35

What The Evidence Suggests 47

Consistency With The Framework 51

Projections 56

Where Dimensions Meet Technology 62

The Final Plan 65

The Comprehensive Framework 73

Appendix 82

   Brain-Computer Interfaces And Higher Dimensions 82

   The Nature Of Heaven In Tanach 88

   Explanations Of The Existence Of The Universe
   Without Creation By God 99

   Quantum Nature Of Time 103

   The Concept Of God Accessing All Of History
   Simultaneously 105

   Overview of Computer-Aided Telepathy 110

   Time Travel Possibilities 114

   Theoretical Frameworks for Consciousness
   and Higher Dimensions 119

   Frequency Of Occurrence Of ESP Phenomena 124

   Edgar Cayce Profile 126

The Free Will vs. Divine Foreknowledge Paradox 128

Prophecy In Deuteronomy 28 133

Scriptural Assertions As To Why
God Created The Universe 135

Scriptural View Of The Interaction Of
Heaven And Earth 137

Scriptural Sources For "The Universe Was Created
For The Sake Of Humanity" 140

Logical Principle Supporting
Sinai Revelation Credibility 144

Scriptural Sources For Concept That God
Continuously Creates Or Sustains The Universe 148

Overview of Mind Uploading Research 153

Fallow Lands And Bumper Crops 159

Skills That Humans Lack At Birth,
That Other Animals Have 162

Merging Of Souls And Minds 168

Basic Physical Constants And "Goldilocks Zones" 171

Higher Dimensions And Noah's Ark And
The Ark Of The Covenant 177

Moshiach's Tasks 179

INTRODUCTION

As I mentioned in my earlier work, ***Believe? Why?***,

> *"Sooner or later, any thinking person ponders the*
> *Great Questions: Who am I? How did I come to be?*
> *How did the world come to be? What is the purpose of*
> *my existence? How can I know that God exists?"*

Sooner seems to have gone by, and Later consequently appears to be now, so I guess this is the time to face these questions.

As I also said in my previous work,

> *Please do not be offended by my writing "God"*
> *rather than "G-d" or "Hashem" (Heb.: "The Name")*
> *as is customary among many Orthodox Jews. The way*
> *I learned it, we must avoid writing any of God's actual*
> *names so as to avoid the possibility of desecrating them.*
> *But God's actual names are Hebrew names, and "God"*
> *is an English name, hence, as I have read it, it is not*
> *really a problem to write "God". I am adopting this*
> *convention as a matter of familiarity for my intended*
> *audience.*

Although this essay is being written from a Jewish perspective, it's intended for anyone of any faith who is interested in a different view of how God relates to the world, from what one might ordinarily receive. The analysis is based mostly on face-value readings of evidence considered, rather than looking for deeply concealed "secret" interpretations. If this piques your interest and you are not Jewish, I recommend you look into the Bnai Noach (or Bnei Noach, "Children of Noah") movement. These are people interested in what guidance Torah provides for all humanity.

The last question on that list, about the existence of God, has a Bottom Line answer which is that one can never really "know" that God exists in the same way that he knows how many fingers he has. However, there are systematic ways he can form a belief about the matter, such as in the way he does in serious situations like jury trials, i.e., by weighing relevant evidence in as unbiased way as possible, and arriving at an honest conclusion. Yes, being "unbiased" is the hard part.

Also as I've said previously:

> *If there is no God, then obviously the very first assertion about Him in the Bible, that He created the universe, would necessarily be false. That would mean that all things in existence are a consequence of a long, if not endless, sequence of random and uncontrolled events, or accidents. Everything that exists other than those things brought into being by the action of Man would exist purely as the result of unintentional happenstance. Even the laws of physics themselves, which govern how all things behave, would also be the results of essentially random interactions of relevant factors.*

It seems to me that if one wishes to subscribe to that belief, then he is faced with the necessity of taking it on faith that such a chain of random events could produce the world as we know it. Or else he needs to rely on scientific investigations to logically arrive at the current physical state of the world, except such a chain of logic ultimately must rely on some set of unprovable axioms. Again, we're stuck with relying on taking some basic things on faith. So, based on the evidence I've observed and discussed in my earlier work, including some events in my own life which seem to me otherwise inexplicable, I'll go with a working principle that God does, indeed exist. I say "working principle" because I don't want to be so arrogant as to think that I can't be wrong.

TRYING TO KNOW GOD

The next question that might come to mind is, "Who or What is God?" Manifestly, the answer to that is actually unknowable. That's because, even according to Divinely revealed information, however tentative at this point it may be, He exists outside or beyond our physical universe. That information, i.e., the Bible, explicitly told us that He created the universe; in fact, it's the very first thing that this information tells us. That directly implies that His existence is outside of our universe, and in some sense, actually preceded it.

This brings the question, *"What is the difference between our universe and the environment of God's existence?"* This introduces a concept with the name "Heaven". Much has been written and said about it, but after all is said and done, it remains an elusive abstract idea. In the Bible, it's sometimes clearly referring to the sky, but at other times, it appears to have something to do with the abode of spiritual entities, such as angels. It's probably reasonable to infer that to the people who first received the Bible, there may have seemed to be no difference between those two. After all, looking up at the sky and not being aware of such things as outer space, that could have been a reasonable conclusion for those people. What we essentially believe about it in more recent times has to do with how it functions in relation to serving the requirements of God and providing an environment for another ephemeral entity, the Soul.

A GLIMPSE INTO HEAVEN

It wasn't that I was particularly searching for some physical analog model for understanding the relationship between our universe and Heaven, but the course of my life seems to have allowed me to arrive at one; one that turns out to enable me to find answers to various related questions.

This vision of a physical-like concept of Heaven began many years ago when I was in high school. In my math class, the teacher went off on a bit of a tangent one day and he described the contents of a book called *Flatland* by Edwin Abbott Abbott, written in 1884 (yes, his middle and last names were the same). The full name of the book is *Flatland: A Romance Of Many Dimensions.* Back then, the term "romance" just meant what we today call a "novel", rather than a courtship-type relationship. If you have already read this book, then you probably also know where I'm going with the ideas it presents.

But if not, please allow me to present an introduction. It's written in the first person from the perspective of an inhabitant of a universe totally different from our own. This universe is what you know from your geometry classes as a plane, one of indeterminate extent. I.e., it's essentially a huge tabletop, except with nothing below supporting it, and nothing above it. The inhabitants of this universe-in-a-plane are geometric shape figures, e.g., triangles, squares, pentagons, etc. The putative author of the narrative is a square, identifying himself as A. Square, and his world as Flatland.

The narrative itself has two broad concepts to present. One is a satire on the Victorian society of his time, with its elitism, class consciousness, hereditary privilege, sexism, and closed mindedness. The other concept explores the effect of exposure to the possibility of other dimensions on one accustomed only to his own.

A good deal of the beginning of the book is a description of what it is like to exist in a planar, i.e., two-dimensional, world in terms to which one in our world can relate.

For example:

> *Place a penny on the middle of one of your tables in Space; and leaning over it, look down upon it. It will appear a circle.*

> *But now, drawing back to the edge of the table, gradually lower your eye (thus bringing yourself more and more into the condition of the inhabitants of Flatland), and you will find the penny becoming more and more oval to your view, and at last when you have placed your eye exactly on the edge of the table (so that you are, as it were, actually a Flatlander) the penny will then have ceased to appear oval at all, and will have become, so far as you can see, a straight line.*

> *The same thing would happen if you were to treat in the same way a Triangle, or Square, or any other figure cut out of pasteboard. As soon as you look at it with your eye on the edge on the table, you will find that it ceases to appear to you a figure, and that it becomes in appearance a straight line. Take for example an equilateral Triangle—who represents with us a Tradesman of the respectable class. Fig. 1 represents the Tradesman as you would see him while* 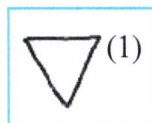 *you were bending over him from above; figs. 2 and 3 represent the Tradesman, as you would see him if your eye were close to the level, or all but on the level of the table; and if your eye were quite on the level of the table*

*(and that is how we see him in Flatland) you would see
nothing but a straight line.*

There is a lengthy discussion of how the inhabitants of this
world interact in their society with each other and even
recognize each other, given that they appear to each other only
as line segments. In these descriptions, you would be able to
see the Victorian society satires.

The discussion of the day-to-day interactions among the
inhabitants of Flatland subtly brings out a point about how the
thinking and viewpoints of these individuals are constrained
and limited by the nature of their environment. Due to the two
dimensional nature of Flatland, the vast majority of inhabitants
are unable to conceive of a third dimension and are stridently
skeptical of any suggestion that such a thing might exist.

The story reaches a point where the narrator, the square, begins
to experience phenomena unlike anything he has encountered
before. First, he hears someone speaking to him, but there
is no one anywhere near him to be the source of the voice.
The speaker tries to explain that it is an occupant of the third
dimension, outside of Flatland, called Spaceland. Try as he
might, the speaker is unable to make the narrator understand
what the third dimension is. The language of Flatland simply
doesn't have words to adequately convey the necessary
concepts, since, indeed, the concepts don't actually exist in
Flatland society or culture.

The speaker then decides to perform a demonstration.
Suddenly, a circle appears out of nowhere near the narrator.
The narrator asks what's going on, and the speaker explains
that he has moved so that he is now intersecting the plane
of Flatland. The narrator can make no sense of the concept
that he is witnessing the result of a slice of the Flatland plane
through the solid body of the speaker. The speaker makes

more movements and the size of the circle changes, further
mystifying the narrator.
The speaker identifies himself as a sphere, and tries to explain
the relationship between a two-dimensional circle and a three-
dimensional sphere, but in vain. Finally, out of frustration,
the sphere grabs the square and pulls him out of Flatland into
Spaceland, in an attempt to make the square understand the
nature of this third dimension. As you might expect, the square
finds this a confusing and traumatizing experience.

> *Once more we ascended into space. "Hitherto,"
> said the Sphere, "I have shewn you naught save Plane
> Figures and their interiors. Now I must introduce you to
> Solids, and reveal to you the plan upon which they are
> constructed. Behold this multitude of moveable square
> cards. See, I put one on another, not, as you supposed,
> Northward of the other, but ON the other. Now a
> second, now a third. See, I am building up a Solid by a
> multitude of Squares parallel to one another. Now the
> Solid is complete, being as high as it is long and broad,
> and we call it a Cube. (1)"*

> *"Pardon me, my Lord," replied I; "but to my eye the
> appearance is as of an Irregular Figure (2) whose inside
> is laid open to the view; in other words, methinks I see no
> Solid, but a Plane such as we infer in Flatland; only of
> an Irregularity which betokens some monstrous criminal,
> so that the very sight of it is painful to my eyes."*

(1)   (2)

After the square is returned to Flatland, the rest of the story chronicles all of the difficulties he encounters when he tries to explain what he has encountered to a highly unreceptive public, even including his own family. He is regarded as being mad or even criminal; he is finally imprisoned.

Flatland uses higher dimensions as an allegory for a spiritual reality beyond human perception. The novella, written by a theologian, criticizes religious institutions that suppress curiosity while framing a search for the divine as a pursuit of greater understanding through faith and imagination.

Although the intent of the author of *Flatland* might not have been to suggest a relationship between our concrete world and any possible higher dimension, the thing about *Flatland* that attracted my attention was the description of the perception and action capabilities that the sphere in Spaceland had in comparison to those of the inhabitants of Flatland.

In addition to being able to provide a voice whose source could not be discerned by a Flatlander, his third dimensional world apparently provided light to the world of Flatland, which source was something of a mystery, as once mentioned by the square. The sphere could simultaneously see both the insides and outsides of objects in Flatland, and could "touch" the insides of the Flatlanders' bodies. The sphere could intersect the plane of Flatland, thereby appearing as a shadow or projection of himself in the form of a circle in the world of Flatland.

ACTUAL DIMENSIONS

By the time I first read Flatland in high school, I had gained some exposure to the ideas underpinning Einstein's Theory of Relativity due to a long standing fascination and interest in science as I grew up. Particularly, I became familiar with the concept that time, when described mathematically, has essentially the same properties as any of the three space dimensions, up-down, left-right, forward-back. In fact, the universe is characterized in this theory as a Four-Dimensional Space-Time Continuum. In trying to explain this concept to someone not already familiar with it, I can well relate to the difficulty that the sphere had in explaining his nature to the square.

Start by imagining a scene containing a group of people walking. The passage of time would be represented by having another scene, depicting the result of that passage of time, showing the people having moved. A further passage of time would be shown as another such scene, with the people having moved a bit more.

A long extent of time would be represented as a succession of many such scenes. This would be analogous to a film strip (assuming that technology isn't too obsolete for you to understand what it was) containing a succession of frames, each depicting one of those scenes. Now, imagine that the frames on that film strip are not the usual two-dimensional photographs of the scenes, but they are the actual three-dimensional scenes themselves. Obviously we're now talking about a very large film strip. Additionally, each frame represents the scene in a particular instant of time, and each successive frame represents the scene in a successive instant of time. Now, the instants of time corresponding to the real world would be infinitesimally close to each other. This provides a vision of the scenes existing in a space-time continuum, except this visualization conceptualizes time as a kind of physical space film strip.

Now, we truly need to strain our imagination and visualize the three dimensional scenes-frames are strung together along a line of time rather than a line of space, which was previously represented by a film strip. The scenes-frames are separated by infinitesimally thin extents of time, thus forming a continuous stream. This is a way to visualize a space-time continuum. This continuum now contains three space dimensions and one time dimension, i.e., it's a four-dimensional space-time continuum.

Now for the really big stretch: imagine that the scenes we've been mentioning are not just limited dioramas, but each one is the entire universe in a particular instant of time! In other words, the universe exists as a cosmic scale four-dimensional space-time continuum. This is what the Theory of Relativity tells us, based on the fact that mathematically, time can be expressed as if it were another dimension of space. E.g., in its simplest case, a difference in time might be expressed as $(t_2 - t_1)$, just as a difference in distance would be expressed as $(x_2 - x_1)$.

Note: This visualization of scene-frames representing instants of time, separated by infinitesimal intervals, means that separating them this way assumes a quantized concept of time, rather than a purely continuous one. Modern theoretical physical theories do give some support for this quantum-time vs. continuous-time view.

Where do we fit in with this picture of the universe? Our consciousness of the "present" is essentially our occupancy of one of those scene-frames at any particular instant. In the next instant, our consciousness migrates into the next scene-frame, and so on.

This concept of the universe, now viewed through the lens of Flatland's ideas about how inhabitants of a higher dimensional world might interact with those of a lower dimensional one, prompted me to consider how such thoughts might relate to reality. It immediately occurred to me that people in our four-dimensional space-time world might have difficulty in conceiving of higher dimensions, just as the square did in Flatland. But even so, the square was still open to the idea of higher dimensions through analogy reasoning:

> *Your Lordship tempts his servant to see whether he remembers the revelations imparted to him. Trifle not with me, my Lord; I crave, I thirst, for more knowledge. Doubtless we cannot SEE that other higher Spaceland now, because we have no eye in our stomachs. But, just as there WAS the realm of Flatland, though that poor puny Lineland Monarch could neither turn to left nor right to discern it, and just as there WAS close at hand, and touching my frame, the land of Three Dimensions, though I, blind senseless wretch, had no power to touch it, no eye in my interior to discern it, so of a surety there is a Fourth Dimension, which my Lord perceives with the inner eye of thought. And that it must exist my Lord himself has taught me. Or can he have forgotten what he himself imparted to his servant?*

> *In One Dimension, did not a moving Point produce a Line with TWO terminal points?*

In Two Dimensions, did not a moving Line produce a Square with FOUR terminal points?

In Three Dimensions, did not a moving Square produce—did not this eye of mine behold it—that blessed Being, a Cube, with EIGHT terminal points?

And in Four Dimensions shall not a moving Cube— alas, for Analogy, and alas for the Progress of Truth, if it be not so—shall not, I say, the motion of a divine Cube result in a still more divine Organization with SIXTEEN terminal points?

Behold the infallible confirmation of the Series, 2, 4, 8, 16: is not this a Geometrical Progression? Is not this—if I might quote my Lord's own words—"strictly according to Analogy"?

Again, was I not taught by my Lord that as in a Line there are TWO bounding Points, and in a Square there are FOUR bounding Lines, so in a Cube there must be SIX bounding Squares? Behold once more the confirming Series, 2, 4, 6: is not this an Arithmetical Progression? And consequently does it not of necessity follow that the more divine offspring of the divine Cube in the Land of Four Dimensions, must have 8 bounding Cubes: and is not this also, as my Lord has taught me to believe, "strictly according to Analogy"?

Indeed, outside of a very limited collection of science fiction literature, such concepts were absent in the culture of the world at large.

DIMENSIONS AND REALITY

In the recent few decades, the world of theoretical physics has been introduced to a body of thought known as *String Theory*. In an attempt to reconcile otherwise conflicting differences between the theories of relativity and quantum mechanics, among other things, string theory came up with a mathematical model of physical reality that posits the existence of at least 10 physical dimensions. So it seems, at least, that there is *some* basis for considering that the existence of higher dimensions has something to do with the way the universe actually works.

Back to our consciousness, if higher dimensions beyond four dimensions do *not* exist, then once we leave the "present" scene-frame and enter the next one, the previous one just exited will no longer exist, and "future" ones will not come into existence until our consciousness reaches them.

But, if higher dimensions *do* exist, then there is no reason why the past and future scene-frames necessarily should not exist, even without being occupied by a "present" consciousness. In fact the whole point behind the concept of the four-dimensional space-time continuum is that these past and future scene-frames WILL exist *within some higher dimensional framework*. If they do exist, they should in some sense be accessible to entities that reside in those dimensions, just as the objects in Flatland were accessible to the sphere in Spaceland. Also, it's conceivable that the migration of consciousness from one scene-frame to the next might be supported by some mechanism employing the properties of higher dimensions.

Likewise, if a higher dimensional environment is where God "dwells", this suggests that all of the scene-frames (i.e., the events of all times) of the four-dimensional space-time continuum "below" Him would be accessible to Him, as is contended by almost all scriptural literature (I.e., God can access the Past, Present, and Future all simultaneously). So the question becomes: why should we believe that these higher dimensions actually exist?

There are either or both of two bases for believing it:

- Logical necessity following from known phenomena.
- Empirical evidence, inexplicable otherwise.

Insofar as logical necessity might provide a basis, while general relativity describes a four-dimensional space-time, theories like string theory, M-theory, and "brane cosmology" provide a theoretical basis for higher dimensions. These remain speculative, as experimental confirmation is still lacking, but they are mathematically consistent and motivated by attempts to unify gravity with quantum mechanics and other forces. In other words, while these theories do provide a logical framework for believing that the higher dimensions might exist, they do *not* provide a logical *necessity*.

For empirical evidence, the question becomes, what credible and *convincing* evidence exists? We would prefer to have rigorous scientific evidence, such as provided by double-blind controlled studies, or by, say, astronomical observations that might clearly show the existence of the hypothesized higher dimension(s). Clearly, no such evidence has ever been produced. The only other kind of evidence that might exist is "anecdotal" evidence, i.e., evidence based on reports of people, usually not well versed in science, of particular items or events that they alone have observed, such as UFO sightings.

Unfortunately, anecdotal evidence has received a rather bad rap. Have you ever tried to make a point with some social science professional, only to be told something like, "*Well, that's just based on anecdotal evidence; it's not scientific; we can't rely on that.*"? Usually, that kind of reply was intended to make you feel like a fool and get you to shut up. And if you didn't understand this dynamic, it probably worked.

Well, I'm here to tell you that you don't have to be a victim of this kind of mind-abuse trap. First, you need to be aware of just what "anecdotal evidence" is.

These are simply statements that purport to be true, which are based on limited or no evidence beyond the testimony of those making the statements, reported by sources that may or may not have some political or economic agenda intended to influence you to believe the object of their agenda. Based on this, you could well believe that the social science professional had a good point after all. Indeed, we would tend to believe scientifically derived information, e.g., results of randomized double-blind studies in which particular hypothesized ideas are applied to one group but not to another control group, and any differences are analyzed. And clearly, this kind of information should be considered as more believable than what I've described as anecdotal information.

That's the ideal. But what happens in real life? In real life, you are continually faced with having to make decisions, some of which will have the profoundest effects on your life or the life of others. For example:

- What kind of work should you do to sustain your very existence?
- Where should you live?
- Whom should you marry?
- If in a judicial proceeding against an individual, what verdict should you find?
- How should you plan for unexpected difficulties?

For any of these, or a multitude of others, were you able to set up some scientific experiment to evaluate all of the possible alternatives and select the best one? Of course not! But upon what DID you actually base your decisions? You based them on whatever facts you could gather relevant to each situation at hand. You analyzed these facts as best as you could and then reached your decisions.

These facts were all anecdotal evidence. As I described above, they came from various sources of all kinds, and you had to evaluate how dependable any of them were. This is the core of the matter: what is the basis for believing anecdotal facts that are presented to us? After all, based on this, it's clear that anecdotal evidence can be crucial in affecting one's life.

This is actually all part of the process of being an executive over one's own life. A business executive once told me, *"Any fool can reach a good decision if he has all the necessary facts, but a good executive routinely makes good decisions based on insufficient data."* **Insufficient data is the normal condition of real life**.

There is an entire branch of philosophy called Epistemology which deals precisely with this issue of how things are known and why things should or should not be believed. I don't intend to present a treatise on epistemology here. I'd just like to present some ideas I've gleaned over the years on practical steps that can help in this regard.

First, you need to be aware that the vast majority of things you believe are things that someone told you. Usually those "someones" would be parents and teachers, but also friends and other acquaintances. Also, of course, there would be all kinds of sources in your culture, e.g., books, news media, music, entertainment, on and on.

Then, you get to believe things you find from your own investigations and explorations. So, what do you believe, and what do you reject, and why?

- Your first sources of beliefs are your parents and teachers. While you are very young, you trust them because they provide you with nurture and protection. Later, you evaluate what you are told by comparing what you are told by one source against what you are told by other sources and by what you observe for yourself. But the point here is, you tend to believe information that comes from sources in whom you've developed trust, either because they've consistently provided you with benefit, or because they have a good track record of giving you information that has held up in the light of other information.

- Next comes corroboration. If you receive anecdotal information from multiple independent sources, ones that you believe are not in collaboration with each other, you would tend to accept that the information is true. Otherwise, you would have to believe that all of these independent sources are wrong together, which would normally be very unlikely.

- Next would be your own investigations. Naturally, you will tend to trust yourself and believe your own observations. But even here, you need to be aware of your own biases and the possibility that observational tricks, such as optical illusions, could be at play.

- Finally comes analysis of the new information in the light of things already known and believed, and in the light of logic. Here is where experience and expertise comes in. If the new information squares with things you already know and/or can derive logically, you will tend to believe it.

That's pretty much it. We do the best we can to make sense of the world based on all of the anecdotal evidence that we are receiving all the time. Unfortunately, sometimes we reach the wrong conclusions: we pick the wrong employment, we live in the wrong place, we marry the wrong person. *"It ain't what we don't know that gets us into trouble; it's what we do know that just ain't so."* (attributed to Artemus Ward, *et al*) I suppose no one is immune to this, but the point is, this is the world in which we live, and the world in which we need to be prepared to apply grains of salt.

And, just to make things a little worse, there can also be problems even with scientific evidence. For one thing, one needs to be aware of who is sponsoring any particular scientific study. It's usually not surprising if a study just happens to confirm the agenda of the organization that sponsors it. Also, many years ago, I saw an article that said a scientific study showed that some 25% of scientific studies were based on faked or doctored data. If this were true, that would mean that that study itself had a 25% chance of being fake. That brings us to the old conundrum *"All generalizations are false, including this one."*

And this has been recognized on a global scale: *"History is the set of lies upon which people agree."* (attributed to Napoleon). So it would seem that one should always be careful about what one chooses to believe.

VALIDITY AND RELIABILITY

How can we recognize if any particular piece of anecdotal evidence might be more valid and reliable than some other one? First, we need to nail down what is meant by "validity" and "reliability"; they are not the same thing. These terms have rigorously separate meanings within statistical analysis, but the differentiation carries into common language.

"Validity" means essentially consistency with truth. I.e., a statement is valid if it makes a statement that is "true" or in some sense can be shown, e.g., by experiment, correctly to represent reality. "Reliability", on the other hand, means that given a particular set of facts, they will always produce the same results when those facts are applied to the situation. For example, if people fail to pay their taxes, the government will reliably go after them to collect the taxes. This can be true even if the citizen actually does not owe the taxes, in which case the tax collection activity will be reliable, but not valid. This is a good example of the difference between reliability and validity.

The terms "validity" and "reliability" are closely related to the terms "accuracy" and "precision". To illustrate this, consider four targets shown here. Shots are fired at the targets and the results are these:

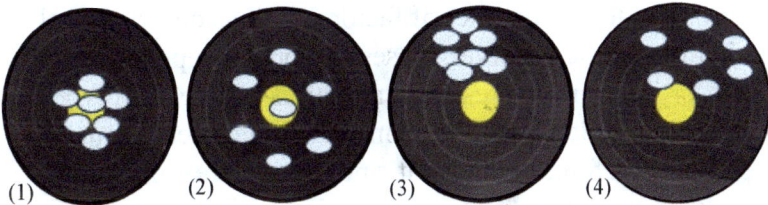

The hits on target #1 are accurate and precise, i.e., they closely cluster around the intended target center, the bullseye; those on target #2 are accurate but not precise, i.e., they center on the bullseye, but are loosely clustered; those on target #3 are precise but not accurate; those on target #4 are neither accurate nor precise. I.e., the accurate hits are, on average, centered on the bullseye even if not closely spaced; the precise hits are all closely positioned together, even if not correctly centered on the bullseye. To be both accurate and precise, the hits must on average be centered on the bullseye and also be closely spaced together.

Likewise, the accurate hits can be considered "valid", since they center on the "true" target object, that is, the bullseye. Also, the precise hits can be considered "reliable" since they all hit the same close area each time, even if that area might not be the bullseye.

In our search for trustworthy anecdotal evidence for the existence of higher dimensions, we will probably find that this evidence will tend to be high in reliability but not so much in validity. For example, we can find many reports of UFO sightings which are very similar to each other, indicating that these sightings can be counted as reliable. However, we cannot ascertain from the details in these reports whether these sightings validly indicate that they represent spacecrafts from extraterrestrial aliens, or, for that matter, artifacts from higher dimensions.

Due to the fact that any particular anecdotal report is subject to error due to any number of factors, such as observational limitations of the observer, biases and preconceptions of the observer, peer group pressures, attention-getting desires, etc., it's highly problematic to rely on very limited sets of such reports. Therefore, I believe, it's necessary to examine the totality of a large body of such anecdotal evidence reports, and there are certain characteristics among these reports to be sought:

1. Reports should come from numerous independent and unconnected sources.

2. Reports should be high in mutual consistency with other independent and unconnected reports, and very low in mutual contradictions.

3. Reports should be high in consistency with known accepted information.

4. Reports should come from sources with very high known credibility and exceptional credentials.

5. Reports should come from sources known not to have political or intellectual agendas, or otherwise biased tendencies.

6. Reports should be relevant to some issue other than the one about which the hypothesis at hand is being examined. E.g., a prophetic insight regarding a moral issue might, apparently coincidentally, have some aspect that has a bearing on the question of higher dimensions. This, again, is a possible indication of lack of bias.

7. Reports with what's known in the lawyers' world as "declarations against interest" should be given special consideration. These are reports where the observer is apparently "testifying against himself" in some fashion, in which situation one would normally be expected not to provide false testimony. It's conceivable that someone might make a "self-incriminating" statement in order to make some other supposedly more important false statement believable, but this would be a very improbable condition.

8. Reports should be given credibility if they come from sources which, if otherwise giving false reports, would immediately be apparent to other numerous observers who could contradict the original reporter. This would usually be the case about any false reports involving natural disasters whose true effects would be known to many other observers.

9. Reports, if possible, should have characteristics inconsistent with having been fabricated by their own known sources. E.g., a peer-reviewed scientific paper presumably couldn't pass peer-review if it were fabricated; it could, however, still be in error if, in an unlikely event, the same error were not detected by the peers.

Obviously no one anecdotal evidence report is likely to have all, or even most, of these characteristics, but again, the point is to be able to consider the totality of the evidence in the light of how the collection of the individual components stack up against these requirements. Given that no credible scientific evidence arises to support the existence of dimensions, spatial or otherwise, beyond the four-dimensional space-time continuum, we are faced with examining the possibly relevant anecdotal evidence, particularly regarding phenomena which cannot otherwise be explained by known science.

WHERE EVIDENCE STARTS TO POINT

One such possibly relevant area is the phenomenon of *quantum entanglement*. Here, particles of atomic or sub-atomic size are able to transmit quantum state information to each other either instantly or very nearly instantly over very long distances, in apparent violation of the known rule in the Theory of Relativity that nothing containing information can travel faster than the speed of light. This cannot be accounted for by any known theory in physics. One possible explanation is that the information is somehow transmitted by jumping from one place in the four-dimensional space-time continuum to another by transiting through a yet higher dimension. Since the higher dimension is outside of the time dimension, the jump appears to take no time, or at least far less time than would be necessary if the speed of light were its limit.

One mechanism by which such a thing could be possible centers on the concept that time is another dimension like space. Start by imagining a cube with a vertical axis around which the cube can rotate. Its "floor" is a plane characterized

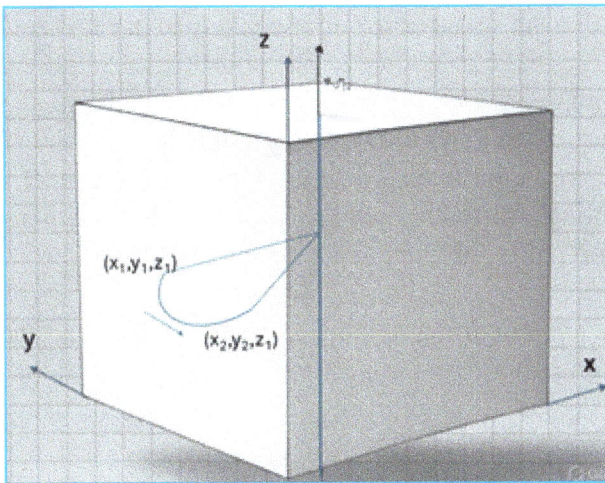

by coordinates x and y. Perpendicular to that is the vertical dimension, with z coordinates. Any point "above" the "floor" has positive z coordinate values, and resides in another plane, parallel to the "floor", and also having x and y coordinates.

If a point within the cube has coordinates (x_1, y_1, z_1) and the cube rotates around the z-direction rotational axis, but still with its "floor" in its same x-y plane, the new coordinates of the point would be (x_2, y_2, z_1). I.e., the coordinate transformation would be expressed as $(x_1, y_1, z_1) \rightarrow (x_2, y_2, z_1)$.

Note that although the x and y coordinates change (have new values, characterized by different subscripts), the z coordinate does not change, since the rotational motion of the cube as a whole does not involve any motion of the point in the vertical, z direction.

Back in Flatland, imagine that there was an Einstein figure who came up with a Theory of Relativity describing a three-dimensional plane-time continuum. I.e., the third dimension would be *time* rather than Spaceland. The three dimensions could be represented by a cube: again start by imagining the cube with a vertical axis around which the cube can rotate. Its "floor" is a plane characterized by coordinates x and y (i.e., the original Flatland). Perpendicular to that is the vertical dimension, with **t** coordinates. Any point "above" the "floor" has positive **t** coordinate values, and resides in another plane representing a different, i.e., future, instant in time, parallel to the "floor", also having x and y coordinates.

Now we are imagining that the t direction defines a time dimension rather than a space dimension. The rotational coordinate transformation around the vertical axis would now be expressed as $(x_1, y_1, t_1) \rightarrow (x_2, y_2, t_1)$.

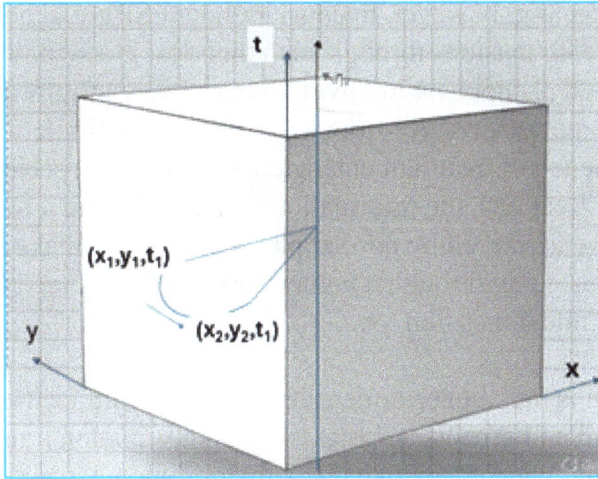

Again, the rotational motion of the cube as a whole does not involve any motion of the point in the vertical, now t direction. The effect would be a movement of the point in its x-y plane from one place to another *with no motion in the (vertical) t direction, i.e., a movement from one place to another in its plane, within its "instant", with no passage of time!* This is just one speculation about how it can be possible for something to move from one place to another in space without any passage of time, taking advantage of relevant characteristics of higher dimensions.

Another possibly relevant area of evidence is Extra Sensory Perception (ESP). This covers a variety of phenomena, including clairvoyance, telepathy, precognition, past-life memory, out-of-body experience, reincarnation, apparitions and even prophecy. This area has relevance because theories like string theory, brane cosmology, and speculative quantum consciousness models propose higher dimensions as a potential framework for ESP, but, of course, these ideas remain unproven and highly speculative.

It's interesting, however, to consider how ESP could be related to higher dimensions through such theories. Precognition and other such phenomena involving transmission of information across time, particularly from the future, share similarity to the phenomenon of quantum entanglement. That is, it seems that in both situations, the information is transmitted in a way that cannot be described by normal physics, but does make sense if viewed as going through a higher dimension, divorced from the normal time dimension.

The idea is that higher-dimensional spaces could facilitate non-local and especially instantaneous information transfer, explaining phenomena like telepathy or remote viewing, or even quantum entanglement itself. Higher dimensions might provide a "medium" for such interactions, bypassing classical spacetime limitations. This information transfer would bypass spacetime limitations because they would be taking place in a higher dimension, one outside of the time dimension of our own four-dimensional space-time continuum. Such information transfer may or may not involve quantum mechanical phenomena, i.e., just the higher dimension(s) alone could be sufficient.

The existence of the phenomenon of ESP is not in question. Occurrences of ESP incidents are so common that even if you haven't been involved in one yourself, you probably are acquainted with someone who has. Usually these incidents are brief and fraught with ambiguity as to how they should be interpreted. Sometimes they are not. Of particular interest is the life of Edgar Cayce (pronounced KAY-see, 1877–1945) who was an American psychic and "Sleeping Prophet", known for giving highly explicit parapsychological readings while in a trance state, covering topics such as health, spirituality, and past lives. He provided over 14,000 readings to thousands of people, offering diagnoses and treatments for illnesses, as well as insights into spiritual and philosophical questions, details of which are well documented.

That he could do these things is beyond doubt. The mystery is just how he did it. While in his sleep-trances, he could receive requests from all kinds of people, for all kinds of information, and he could receive relevant information to provide satisfactory responses to the requests made of him. The mechanism by which he could do this has never been explained in terms of known science.

There is a plethora of anecdotal evidence, most of which satisfies, one way or another, the first 6 criteria in the list above. The question is, evidence of what? This is where theories and hypotheses come in. These are collections of statements or ideas that purport to explain observed phenomena, but also, it's desired for them to validly and reliably predict how newly-observed phenomena will connect to other phenomena that are subject to observation and verification.

Back to *Flatland*. As mentioned earlier, the main point of the story was to provide a satire on the intolerant attitudes of the cultural institutions of the Victorian era in which the author lived. I'm not sure if the author actually intended to present the relationship between Flatland and Spaceland as an allegory of the relationship between the Earth and Heaven, but that's how it immediately struck me when I first read the work. The capabilities of the sphere in dealing with the two dimensional world of the square instantly reminded me of the traditional descriptions of how God interacts with, and relates to our world.

It didn't take much of a leap to see that the sphere's relationship with Flatland, especially his abilities to "reach down" to touch and control a variety of objects in Flatland, was highly reminiscent of descriptions of God's interactions with the Earth and human society, with miracles such as the Flood and the Plagues of Egypt, and rendering prophetic messages to select individuals as required.

SIGNIFICANCE OF
HIGHER DIMENSIONS

The question then became, if it seems like God's domain is a higher dimensional space, then so what? Of what importance would that be? For a long time I set that question aside. While I was not religious, that question, indeed, had no importance for me. Once I did become religious, as referenced above, I was faced with the availability of a plethora of scriptural literature, comprising a huge body of anecdotal evidence about the existence and activities of God. In order to come to a comprehensive framework of thought enabling a coherent understanding of all of this material, I desired to adopt some picture of an ordered background of how it all could fit together. I, of course, concede that this picture is highly speculative, but I believe it does provide the coherent understanding that I sought.

That's where the picture of the relationship of entities in a higher dimensional world with those in a lower dimensional one, as presented in *Flatland*, came to mind. If this picture could provide a comprehensive understanding of how the environment of God might be related to the environment of the world, what other understandings could it provide? That's the point of having a theory to explain phenomena. The more phenomena it can explain, the better the theory would be considered, provided, of course, no irrefutable contradictory facts arise. The phenomena in question here are the anecdotal reports of actions by, or related to, God.

Before attempting to examine how well the theory handles these reports, we need to consider how valid and reliable these reports are in the first place, in view of the list of desirable characteristics for anecdotal evidence given above.

The bulk of anecdotal evidence about God and His relationship to Earth and Man would be, of course, scriptural writing of various religions. Since I am Jewish, I am most familiar with the scriptures of Judaism, but also with other religions, primarily Christianity, and to a lesser extent Islam, therefore, it's the information in these scriptures that provides most of the anecdotal evidence I would use for analyses relevant to the theory I want to develop. This scriptural literature would not be limited to Bibles, but could include auxiliary philosophical discourses and commentaries as well.

From what I have seen, the Bibles and other scriptural literature of Christianity and Islam concentrate on people and events on Earth along with the influences that God has on them. Issues of the nature of God, Himself, or Heaven seem to have secondary focus. The Jewish scriptures are the "Old Testament" (*Tanach*, in Hebrew, starting with the Pentateuch, which are also called The Five Books Of Moses, continuing with books of the Prophets, Psalms, Proverbs and other narratives), the Talmud (containing explanatory and supplementary information from the "Oral Torah", given by God orally to Moses on Mt. Sinai, plus analyses and commentaries on the Oral Torah), plus other commentary literature that came after the Talmud. (The term "Torah" is flexible, sometimes referring only to the Pentateuch, and at other times referring to any or all of the rest; its meaning depends on the context of its usage.) In these, there is rather heavy emphasis on understanding the nature of God in terms of inferences stemming from His Will and activities, especially in the Talmud and other literature. This provides a rich trove of the kind of anecdotal evidence needed for the basis of the theory to be developed.

Other relevant evidence consists of a large body of reports on prophecies and other ESP incidents outside of scriptural purview, such as clairvoyance, telepathy, and precognition mentioned earlier.

The next question is, how do all these pieces of evidence stack up against the list of criteria given above about desirable characteristics for the evidence, contributing to their credibility?

1.   *Reports should come from numerous independent and unconnected sources.*
The vast majority of the evidence is quite good in this regard. The reports come from sources all over the world, both religious and secular, over many years.

2.   *Reports should be high in mutual consistency with other independent and unconnected reports, and very low in mutual contradictions.*
Again, the reports seem good according to this criterion. They tend to be so good, in fact, that critics who wish to deny their validity often assert that the reports are contrived to resemble each other. You, the observer, would need to make your own judgements in this respect. Particularly notable are numerous well documented reports of near-death experiences from many independent sources around the world over long periods of time that closely resemble each other.

3.   *Reports should be high in consistency with known accepted information.*
The reports have high variability in this regard. The researcher would need, on a case-by-case basis, to examine each report to see if the religious or ESP incident produced or predicted results consistent with known outcomes. E.g., did prophecies and precognition events accurately predict events in their respective futures; were clairvoyant events corroborated by relevant observations; could past-life stories be backed up with facts? Sometimes they did; sometimes not.

One particularly good example in this regard were prophecies in Deuteronomy 28, regarding calamities the Nation of Israel was in jeopardy of experiencing were they not to adhere to God's prescriptions. Predictions in Deuteronomy 28 regarding consequences of disregard of the Law and resultant destruction of the Jewish state (which predictions, no one contests, were written well before the destruction of the Second Temple) pose many unusual or unlikely *a-priori* scenarios for such destruction. E.g., it is predicted that the land would be utterly destroyed, cities laid waste, agriculture destroyed, and population completely removed from the land. Conquerors of the era in which those predictions were supposedly written by men presumably without precognition, didn't do business that way – it made no logistic or economic sense, since conquering armies of those times, not having modern-style long supply lines, depended on the produce and labor of people of the lands they conquered. Yet, that prediction is exactly what happened at the time of the destruction of the Second Temple. Also, it was predicted that Israel would be conquered by a people whose language the Jews wouldn't understand and that some of the people would be brought back to Egypt in ships. The most likely people to bring the Jews back to Egypt in ships would have been Egyptians, and the Jews *did* understand their language. So the Bible predicted something quite unlikely. In fact, the Romans conquered Israel, speaking Latin, a language the Jews didn't (at first) understand, and they did happen to deport many of the Jews to Egypt with ships.

4.   *Reports should come from sources with very high known credibility and exceptional credentials.* In this regard, the reports have extremely high variability. They might have come from enormously

highly respected clergy or scientists renowned for their fidelity to the truth, or they might have come from one's frequently inebriated neighbor, or anyone in between. They need to be analyzed on a case-by-case basis. Even with this, though, there is always the possibility that someone normally reliable for expounding the truth could fall victim to some unintentional error.

5.   *Reports should come from sources known not to have political or intellectual agendas, or otherwise biased tendencies.*
There is always a danger that any reports could be subject to biases held by their sources. The sources must always be analyzed to identify what biases they might have. It would be particularly interesting, though, if the conclusions reached in the report somehow go against the known biases of the sources (see #7 below).

6.   *Reports should be relevant to some issue other than the one about which the hypothesis at hand is being examined. E.g., a prophetic insight regarding a moral issue might, apparently coincidentally, have some aspect that has a bearing on the question of higher dimensions. This, again, is a possible indication of lack of bias.*
Virtually none of the evidence reports overtly show aspects that point to connections to higher dimensions. This narrative, however, will attempt to discern if such connections can be inferred in various evidence reports.

7.   *Reports with what's known in the lawyers' world as "declarations against interest" should be given special consideration. These are reports where the source is apparently "testifying against himself" in some fashion, in which situation one would normally be expected not to provide false testimony. It's conceivable*

that someone might make a "self-incriminating" statement in order to make some other supposedly more important false statement believable, but this would be a very improbable condition.

The occurrence of declarations against interest is an extreme rarity in the evidence reports. Normally, a source would just be interested in presenting the information at hand and have it believed at face value or with only routine scrutiny. The Tanach is a glaring exception to this rule.

Tanach often portrays its protagonists with human flaws, highlighting their imperfections to emphasize moral lessons, growth, or the need for divine guidance. Below are key incidents where major figures are shown in a negative light due to character faults, drawn from the text:

Adam and Eve (Genesis 3)
Fault: Disobedience, pride, succumbing to temptation.
Incident: Adam and Eve eat the forbidden fruit from the Tree of Knowledge after being tempted by the serpent, disregarding God's command. Their actions stem from curiosity and a desire for knowledge akin to God's, revealing pride and a lack of trust.

Noah (Genesis 9:20-27)
Fault: Drunkenness, lack of self-control.
Incident: After the flood, Noah, described as a righteous man, plants a vineyard, gets drunk, and lies naked in his tent.

Abraham (Genesis 12:10-20, 20:1-18)
Fault: Fear, deception, lack of faith.
Incident: Twice, Abraham lies about Sarah being

his sister (once to Pharaoh, once to Abimelech), fearing for his life. This endangers Sarah and others, showing a lack of trust in God's protection despite His promises.

Isaac (Genesis 26:6-11)
Fault: Deception, fear.
Incident: Like his father Abraham, Isaac lies about his wife Rebekah being his sister to Abimelech, fearing for his life. This repetition shows an inherited tendency toward deceit under pressure.

Jacob (Genesis 27, 30:25-43)
Fault: Deceit.
Incident: Jacob deceives his father Isaac to steal his brother Esau's blessing, aided by his mother, Rebekah.

Joseph's Brothers, sons of Jacob (Genesis 37)
Fault: Jealousy, hatred, betrayal.
Incident: Driven by envy of Joseph's favored status and dreams, his brothers plot to kill him but instead sell him into slavery, lying to Jacob about his fate.

Moses (Exodus 2:11-12, Numbers 20:7-12)
Fault: Anger, disobedience.
Incident: Early on, Moses kills an Egyptian who was beating a Hebrew, acting impulsively out of anger. Later, at Meribah, he strikes a rock to bring water instead of speaking to it as God commanded, showing frustration and disobedience.

Aaron (Exodus 32)
Fault: Weakness, idolatry, people-pleasing.
Incident: While Moses is on Sinai, Aaron yields to the Israelites' demands and creates a golden calf for

worship, failing to uphold God's commands.

Gideon (Judges 8:22-27)
Fault: Pride, idolatry.
Incident: After leading Israel to victory, Gideon refuses a kingship but creates an ephod from gold, which becomes an object of worship, leading Israel astray.

David (2 Samuel 11-12)
Fault: Coveting another's wife, abuse of power.
Incident: David (apparently) commits adultery with Bathsheba, then orchestrates her husband Uriah's death to cover it up. His actions stem from unchecked desire and a sense of entitlement as king.

Solomon (1 Kings 11)
Fault: Idolatry, disobedience, lust.
Incident: Despite his wisdom, Solomon marries many foreign women who lead him to help them worship their gods, defying God's commands. His pursuit of wealth and alliances overshadows his devotion.

In fairness, commentaries often point out that some of these incidents are portrayed the way they are in the text of the Tanach in order to emphasize the importance of the moral precepts they are intended to highlight, whereas details behind the incidents can present a different perspective. E.g., Jacob and Rebekah conspired to deceive the now-blind Isaac in order to protect him from erroneously giving his valuable blessing to Esau, known by Rebakah and Jacob but not Isaac, to be of villainous character, not deserving of the blessing. Also, in the time of King David, it was customary for soldiers going to war to issue pro-forma divorces to their wives so as to protect them from becoming legally unable to remarry if the husbands were "missing in action", but not verifiably killed in battle. Uriah, the husband of Bathsheba, gave such a divorce to her so that technically, even regardless if he were not killed in a war, David did nothing legally wrong in marrying her. The prophet Nathan convinced David, however, that his actions were unethical, prompting him to repent.

The inclusion of these incidents in Tanach, however, do tend to bolster the credibility of this narrative, since they could just as easily been left out or otherwise been presented in more favorable lights.

8.   *Reports should be given credibility if they come from sources which, if otherwise giving false reports, would immediately be apparent to other numerous observers who could contradict the original reporter. This would usually be the case about any false reports involving natural disasters whose true effects would be known to many other observers.*

This would be an extremely rare characteristic to find in these reports. Normally, natural disasters would be the only kinds of events to which this analysis would apply. There is, however, one historical event other than a natural disaster to which this analysis is also relevant. This was when God came down on Mt. Sinai and appeared before the entire nation of Israel to give the Ten Commandments. Here we have an assertion about **an extremely dramatic traumatically attention-demanding event** (See Exodus 19-20) **occurring before the entire population** of the society of the nation of Israel, which assertion, historically, until only early in the 19th century, was accepted as Truth by the entire society of the Jewish People. According to logical principles, this means that the belief, in itself, is good *evidence* that the event actually did happen. If the revelation at Sinai didn't really happen, there is no way the entire society could have come to accept it, especially the Jews, who have always been noted culturally for being "stiff necked" and skeptical. Moreover, if it didn't happen anyone who might have considered asserting it would have known that it is the kind of falsehood that no one would believe, because it would simply contradict well established common knowledge of the listeners.

This was a dramatic miraculous event, observed by the entire population of the Israelites, and, as importantly, believed by the entire Jewish population up until relatively recent times. All the conditions necessary are present for us to conclude that it actually did happen. Otherwise, we would have to believe that the entire nation of Israel conspired on the spot to adopt this supposedly false story encompassing the entire nation, or that later generations formed a conspiracy for the same purpose. The entire edifice of Judaism rests on the veracity of the proposition that this Revelation actually did occur. Else the entire enterprise of Judaism is based purely on a myth.

9.   *Reports, if possible, should have characteristics inconsistent with having been fabricated by their own known sources. E.g., a peer-reviewed scientific paper presumably couldn't pass peer-review if it were fabricated; it could, however, still be in error if, in an unlikely event, the same error were not detected by the peers.*
Again, it would be very uncommon to find this characteristic in the evidence reports available, however, again, Tanach provides an exception. The

law of *"Shmitah"* is totally inconsistent with having been originated by any known human source, Moses or otherwise:

> *LEVITICUS 25:1 And the Lord spake unto Moses in mount Sinai, saying, 2 Speak unto the children of Israel, and say unto them,* **When ye come into the land which I give you, then shall the land keep a sabbath unto the Lord.** *3 Six years thou shalt sow thy field, and six years thou shalt prune thy vineyard, and gather in the fruit thereof;* **4 But in the seventh year shall be a sabbath of rest unto the land, a sabbath for the Lord: thou shalt neither sow thy field, nor prune thy vineyard. 5 That which groweth of its own accord of thy harvest thou shalt not reap, neither gather the grapes of thy vine undressed: for it is a year of rest unto the land.** *... 8 And thou shalt number seven sabbaths of years unto thee, seven times seven years; and the space of the seven sabbaths of years shall be unto thee forty and nine years. ... 10 And ye shall hallow the fiftieth year, and proclaim liberty ... 11 A* **jubilee shall that fiftieth year be unto you: ye shall not sow, neither reap that which groweth of itself in it, nor gather the grapes in it of thy vine undressed.** *12 For it is the jubilee; it shall be holy unto you: ye* **shall eat the increase thereof out of the field.** *... 20* **And if ye shall say, What shall we eat the seventh year? behold, we shall not sow, nor gather in our increase: 21 Then I will command my blessing upon you in the sixth year, and it shall bring forth fruit for three years.** *22 And ye shall sow the eighth year, and eat yet of old fruit until the ninth year; until her fruits come in ye shall eat of the old store.*

No leaders of human societies would ever, or did ever,

construct rules mandating leaving all farmlands within their sovereign control fallow for a full year. I.e., this law mandates letting all farms in the Land of Israel lie fallow every 7th year and every 50th year and requires dependence on God to supply bumper crops in the years immediately *preceding* the fallow years. And since everyone entered the Land at the same time, everyone observed these sabbatical years jointly with each other. Note: in the 49th and 50th years, all of the farmlands are to be left fallow for *two years in succession*! (Although in the 50th year, they could eat whatever grew by itself.)

If men interested in protecting their own interests and those of people within their responsibility invented this law, they would be exposing themselves to immense risks of loss of credibility, not to mention economic chaos, if their postulated "Will of God" would not back the law up with the expected bumper crops at the "right" times. Of critical importance is the fact that these required times are the *wrong* times, according to the most elementary knowledge of agriculture, which indicates that the bumper crops would come *after* the fallow years, not before. If such men wrote Torah, why on Earth would they include this law? This tends to confirm the contention in the Talmud that Moses did not himself originate the law, but that he received the instructions from God.

WHAT THE EVIDENCE SUGGESTS

If one would look at all of this anecdotal evidence and think that all of it is true, that would certainly not be realistic. It will be possible to find instances where the reports are false. For example, Harry Houdini, the famous escape artist, later in life made a career of exposing fraudulent séance purveyors, of which he found many. But it would be equally illogical to presume that all of the reports are false. We are left with having to apply our own critical analytical skills in looking at them, and basing our further development of a theory to explain where it all points upon those reports that hold up the best against the criteria we have adopted for making these judgments.

Returning to the essential question at hand: how, if at all, does any or all of this evidence support the concept that higher dimensions exist beyond the four dimensional space-time continuum? And if they do, what phenomena are consistent with their existence? In other words, given some reasonable level of validity of this evidence, what logical or rational implications can be discerned by all of this?

We can begin with the huge body of scriptural evidence, specifically with the Tanach, and more specifically, with its beginning, the Book of Genesis, which fittingly enough, deals with the beginnings of the universe, as mentioned above. *"In the beginning, God created the Heaven(s) and the Earth …"* Clearly, this indicates that God existed outside, and in some sense, even before the thing(s) being created. Other than asserting that God is Something capable of doing such a Creation, we are told nothing else about the nature of God, rather, we are told about His actions.

It says that He created two things: the Heaven(s) and the

Earth. In the original Hebrew, the word normally translated as "Heaven" is *Shamayim*, which is a plural form, which is why I have rendered it as "Heaven(s)". This seems to suggest that the Heaven(s) thus created consisted of a multiplicity of components. We can consequently visualize God as having constructed, as it were, a structure consisting of the multi-component Heaven and the Earth, with God being outside of all of this.

This included God being outside of time. We can infer this from how the very first thing that He commanded was "*Let there be light.*" This command inferentially included creation of the physical laws by which light can exist. The existence of light is a fundamental building block of existence of the universe. The theory of Special Relativity tells us that the speed of light, i.e., speed of photon travel, is an invariant constant, the same for all observers regardless of their motion with respect to the source of the light, or each other. Speed is the ratio of distance (space) divided by time. So, by establishing the law for the existence of light, God was also necessarily setting the laws by which both space and time (from His position outside of both) would exist. Moreover, this interpretation is consistent with the fact that no source for any physical light had yet been specified.

Harking back to what was said earlier about Heaven being viewed in Tanach sometimes as the sky, and sometimes as a purely spiritual realm, this "structure" is consistent with that. It is also consistent with a visualization that the Heavens consist of higher spatial dimensions and the "Earth" would, in context, be a euphemism for the four dimensional space-time continuum. And God would, at least to start, be outside of all of that.

We are then told that God spent six "days" creating various

components of the Earth. Clearly, if God created these components from outside of the "Earth", then those "days" could not have been what we experience as days, since they existed outside of the "Earth's" time dimension. Evidently, in the Tanach text, they are a figure of speech used to help ancient people, to whom these scriptures were first given, have a frame of reference meaningful to them. In actuality, they might merely specify the sequence of actions that God used to fashion His Creation, unrelated to any extents of time, since, as we noted, God "operates" outside of time.

The Tanach itself provides a hint confirming this with a phenomenon unique to Biblical Hebrew where, when a letter vav (ו) (which literally translates as "and") is prepended to a verb, that inclusion reverses the verb's tense. This is known as the vav-consecutive (also called *vav ha-hippukh*, "the vav of reversal"). This grammatical feature is unique to Biblical Hebrew and primarily influences the verb's tense or aspect, often "reversing" it, though the precise effect depends on the context and the verb form. For example, the Hebrew statement "*Yhee ohr vyhee ohr*" literally translates as "*Let there be light **and** let there be light*", but its translation in context is "*Let there be light and there **was** light*". This effect occurs all throughout the Tanach, indicating, apparently, that time is a manifestation having some flexibility.

As I mention in my earlier work, I believe that the things being created during these "days" were the physical laws by which the Earth would exist, rather than the explicit things themselves (to be created later, also as explained in the earlier work). For example, contrary to an expectation that the sun should exist before plants would, since the plants depend on sunlight for their existence, the laws for the existence of plants (on "day" 3) precede the laws for the existence of the sun (on "day" 4) because the laws of the plants would include what kind of sunlight should be necessary for their existence, and based on that the laws of the sun could then be developed so that the correct sunlight would be produced, once the plants and the sun would be physically Created. Any actual time involved in these Creation activities becomes irrelevant. It's not until God ordains the laws of Sabbath that time becomes of the essence.

CONSISTENCY
WITH THE FRAMEWORK

At this point we can seek other phenomena that would be consistent with this framework. We noted that consciousness of events in the "present" seems to migrate from one scene-frame in the four dimensional space-time continuum to the next. The exact nature and mechanics of consciousness have long been a tantalizing mystery to science. It requires the human brain for its function, however, brain functions alone don't adequately explain differences in its nature between that in humans vs. that in other living beings.

Specifically, brain functions alone don't account for the use of spoken languages and complex moral codes that are unique to humans. Also, brain functions utterly fail to account for ESP phenomena related to consciousness: telepathy, clairvoyance, precognition, past-life memory, reincarnation and prophecy. (An interesting aspect of prophecy is that in Talmudic literature, it is asserted that the people receiving prophetic visions had those visions come to them while sleeping or otherwise in a trance state. Moses was a unique exception to this, in that he is characterized as receiving his prophetic information while awake "speaking to God face-to-face". These assertions were made millennia ago, yet we also witnessed Edgar Cayce receiving his prophetic information this same exact way in our own times.)

Based on this shared characteristic of ESP phenomena, that it seems to support the transfer of information across and outside the bounds of time, consciousness would seem to be an interface of sorts between the ordinary day-to-day functions of the brain, such as control of the body and thought, and a functionality in a higher dimension, outside of space-time. The combination of consciousness and this higher dimensional functionality is, I believe, what we identify as the soul, based on how the soul is discussed in various scriptural literature.

The basic Bibles contained in the body of anecdotal evidence with which we are working make little reference to the soul as such, however, ancillary material, particularly the Talmud and related commentaries discourse about it extensively. Among the many characteristics analyzed are several relevant to the concepts of how the soul could be placed into the framework of higher dimensional spaces. Primary among these is the assertion that the soul constitutes an essence of an individual human that links his consciousness, personality and character to the realm of Heaven, and that this essence survives physical death and is then preserved in Heaven.

In view of theories that connect consciousness to quantum mechanical processes, and through these, to higher dimensional spaces, it would seem that Heaven would be, in some sense, an edifice that is, at least, analogous to a higher dimensional construct, if not literally such a construct itself. This view of the soul, as a connection between the living human on the Earth, within a four-dimensional space-time continuum, and a "spiritual" component in the higher dimensional Heaven, can help us assemble various puzzle pieces of evidence and assertions about the soul.

First, and probably foremost, it can allow us to understand the mortality of the physical body vs. the purported immortality of the soul. If the spiritual component of the soul exists in a higher dimensional Heaven, then it should be unaffected by time, one of the lower four dimensions. Its behaviors and activities likewise should appear to be unconstrained by time. This is particularly consistent with evidence of reincarnation and past-lives memories. In this view, the spiritual component can move from one four-dimensional space-time scene-frame to another, appearing to occupy one life at one time and another one at another time.

If a soul is capable of moving from one space-time frame to another, then it's not a stretch to consider that it can similarly transmit information from one space-time frame to another. This makes the phenomenon of prophecy easily understandable. I.e., the prophet receives information about times and/or spaces far removed from him when his soul accesses that information through higher dimensional channels. The scriptural literature generally characterizes the prophets as saintly people who receive their prophetic visions in trances or sleep.

There are few exceptions to this: one we already mentioned, being Moses who received his Divine revelations while awake; another is Baalam who received prophetic information (presumably while asleep), but who is described in the scriptural literature as person of poor moral character. A few other individuals are also cited as having received warnings in their dreams against improper behavior, such as Abimelech, king of Gerar, who might have otherwise violated Sarah. Interestingly enough though, a historical search for felons or other nefarious people who have been cited as having had prophetic experiences will turn up essentially blank. This would seem to confirm the contentions in the scriptural literature about the nature of souls, prophecy and prophets.

This concept of the soul functioning as a connection between the human body and a component of the person in a higher dimensional Heaven helps with understanding of various other ESP phenomena:

> • Clairvoyance - The soul receives information about
> remote areas through a higher dimensional information

transmission mechanism.

• Telepathy - Similar to clairvoyance, with information transfer between individuals via a similar mechanism.

• Precognition - Similar to clairvoyance, with information transfer to the individual from his "future" via a similar mechanism.

• Past-life memory - Similar to clairvoyance, with information transfer to the individual from his "past" via a similar mechanism.

• Out-of-body experience - The soul becomes detached from the body, remains conscious, retains memories, and returns to the body. This would seem not necessarily to involve interactions with a higher dimensional Heaven, however the mechanism that makes this possible might have a connection.

• Reincarnation (*Gilgul*, in Hebrew) - After death, the soul resides in the higher dimensional Heaven for some period of time, then re-enters the world in a new human body, usually at birth. If the re-entry occurs at a time when the person is older, it's characterized as a "Possession" (*Dybbuk*, in Hebrew, particularly if having destructive intent). Reports of phenomena like these seem to indicate that while "between" earthly sojourns, the soul does not experience any aging, again confirming the independence from time.

The question arises as to why memories of past lives are not normally available in current lives, but only become accessible through hypnosis and the like. It would seem that the human brain is built only to retain the memories of current life experiences, however, when the soul is "prompted" through hypnosis to access the past life experiences, it apparently can tap into a separate memory repository available to the soul through the higher dimensions.

• Apparitions - This is the phenomenon of "ghosts". It would seem to be rather similar to the Out-Of-Body experience, except that it starts after the soul has left a deceased body, it returns to Earth and is capable of interacting with living persons while they are awake. It's not clear when, how, or even if, such a soul then returns to Heaven or to another earthly host. Again, this would seem not necessarily to involve interactions with a higher dimensional Heaven, however the mechanism that makes this possible might have a connection.

There is a Talmudic assertion that the soul enters the fetus 40 days after conception, which is primarily derived from the Babylonian Talmud, specifically in Yevamot 69b and Menachot 99b. According to these texts, the embryo is considered to be "mere water" (*maya b'alma*) during the first 40 days of gestation, implying it does not yet have the full status of a human life with a soul. After this period, the soul is believed to enter the fetus, marking a significant stage in its development. Modern science has discovered that although the Y-chromosome, which causes a human to be a male, may be present in a fetus at conception, the male physical characteristics that it causes don't begin to manifest themselves until … 40 days after conception, an interesting "coincidence". Presumably the soul would be "on hold" in the higher dimensions until the prescribed time.

PROJECTIONS

An interesting aspect of objects in higher dimensional spaces is that images of themselves can be produced in lower dimensional spaces. This is the process of *projection*. In our world, photographs are common examples of the results of projection. The images of three dimensional objects in the photograph are projections of the objects onto two-dimensional photo print paper.

Projections of higher dimensional objects onto lower dimensional spaces can easily have very diverse appearances. E.g., full face and profile photographs (two dimensional) of a person (three dimensional) look very different from each other. A space alien who never before saw a human might not be able to guess that those two photos are of the same being.

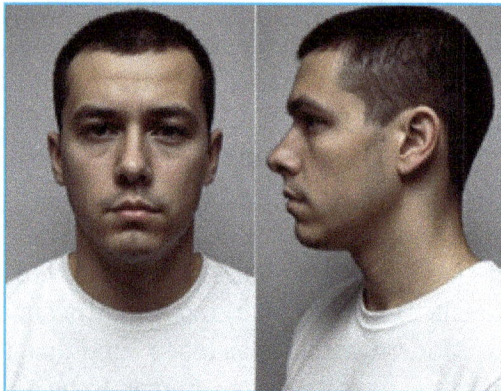

The space alien might say, "Obviously these pictures are of two very different creatures. The one on the left has two eyes, a nose, and a mouth is the middle of the front of its narrow head, and two ears on the sides of its head. The one on the right has only one eye with a nose and a mouth on the side of its wide head, with only one ear in the middle of its head. It's absurd to think that these pictures are of two creatures of the same species, much less the same individual."

This concept can be generalized (ignoring the time dimension for the moment), e.g., a projection of some object existing in a four-dimensional space would, in principle, be able to be projected into our three-dimensional space and appear as a solid three-dimensional object. The actual projection mechanism might be analogous to how photons from the three-dimensional object transmit information to the two-dimensional print paper.

This conception elegantly explains how *"Let Us make man in Our image, after Our likeness"* (Genesis 1:26) happened, yet individual people look different from each other. As shown above, various projections of a higher dimensional Object (i.e., God) onto lower dimensional space can have widely varying appearances (i.e., people).

We can further generalize this concept to visualize a cosmic film projector, where the film is the stream of four-dimensional scene-frames described earlier. Only, when God turns on the projector (like commanding, *"Let there be light"*), the projector does not project a single scene-frame at a time, but rather it projects the entire film strip, all at once. This physically produces the entire universe as it exists throughout all time in one long panorama. Now, we can visualize how God can

access all events in all past, present and future history, all together in a single "glance", rather like how we can look at a passing train and see all of its cars at once.

Just bear in mind that unlike a person looking at a train, God could "reach into" any and all frames at once and manipulate them as He requires. Again, our consciousness occupies one frame at a time, each containing the whole universe at a particular instant of time, and migrates from one frame to the next, in the future.

This begins to suggest how the paradoxical coexistence of Free Will and Divine Foreknowledge could actually be resolved. In its particular instant of time, the consciousness exerts its Free Will to do some action. At that point, God exerts *His* Free Will to determine the outcome of the consciousness' *action* in the next frame and all succeeding frames (thus creating the Divine Foreknowledge, and the capability to direct outcomes to lead to His desired goals). When the consciousness reaches the next frame, this whole process repeats, and again for all succeeding frames. But, since every consciousness in the world is in each frame, we strain to imagine how God can do this for all consciousness' for all time frames, yet, that's what He does!

This projection model is also consistent with assertions in scriptural literature to the effect entities in Heaven and on Earth can have effects on each other, i.e., there could be a two-way projection process among these objects.

This view of the nature of the universe as a somewhat mechanistic projection brings to mind recent conjectures that the universe might actually be some kind of computer simulation. Several modern theories and hypotheses suggest that our world might be a computer simulation, with some of the most prominent being:

1.   Digital Physics: This framework, explored by physicists like John Wheeler and later Konrad Zuse, posits that the universe operates like a giant computational system. The idea of "it from bit" (Wheeler) suggests that reality is fundamentally information-based, and physical processes are akin

to computations. This supports the notion that the universe could be a simulation running on some cosmic computational substrate.

2.   Holographic Principle: Proposed by Gerard 't Hooft and expanded by Leonard Susskind, this principle suggests that the universe's information is encoded on a lower-dimensional boundary, much like a hologram. While not explicitly a simulation theory, it aligns with the idea that reality might be a projection or simulation, as it implies the universe's information content is finite and could be computationally represented.

3.   Quantum Mechanics and Computational Limits: Some interpretations of quantum mechanics, like the observer effect and the apparent "pixelation" of reality at the Planck scale, are cited by simulation theorists as evidence that the universe might operate like a computational system with finite resolution. For example, the work of physicists like David Deutsch and Seth Lloyd explores how quantum computers could simulate complex physical systems, lending credence to the idea that our reality could be a quantum simulation.

4.   Anthropic Principle and Simulation: The anthropic principle, which addresses why the universe seems fine-tuned for life, is sometimes linked to simulation arguments. Some theorists suggest that a simulated universe might be designed with parameters optimized for conscious observers, explaining why physical constants appear finely tuned.

This particular concept actually aligns well with assertions in scriptural literature to the effect that *"the universe was Created for the sake of Man"*.

These theories remain speculative but draw from philosophy, physics, and computer science to argue that our reality could be a sophisticated computational construct. However, these conjectures also align very well with concepts advanced in scriptural literature to the effect that God continuously supports the universe in a process reflecting an ongoing Creation activity. I.e., He supplies "power" to the universe-simulation. This further supports a speculation that "Virtual Reality" and "Real Reality" are not two different things.

If the theory of a multi-dimensional Heaven coherently addresses the various phenomena mentioned in the scriptures, as well as those of ESP, what predictions can it make whose outcomes we would be able to experience? On a personal level, we would need to check what prophecies or ESP encounters predict and verify them on a case-by-case basis. For the broad sweep of history, such prophecies tend to be very non-specific.

There are some fairly specific prophecies regarding the activities of the era of the Messiah (*Moshiach*), and the state of the world at that time and rather shortly after. The results of these activities will be evident and observable by virtually everyone in the world. But, once that period is complete, we enter the "End of Days", and that's where the prophecies become much less specific.

The concept of the End of Days and the state of the world after *Moshiach* has come and completed his work is addressed in various scriptural sources within Judaism, primarily in the Hebrew Bible (Tanach), the Talmud, and other rabbinic literature. These sources provide a vision of the Messianic era and the subsequent period, often referred to as *Olam HaBa* (the World to Come) or the ultimate "End of Days."

Scriptural sources portray the Messianic era as a time of peace, restoration, and universal knowledge of God, with the *Moshiach* rebuilding the Temple and gathering the exiles. The "End of Days" or *Olam HaBa* follows as a spiritual era marked by resurrection, divine judgment, and a new Creation where the righteous dwell eternally with God.

WHERE DIMENSIONS
MEET TECHNOLOGY

What's understandably missing from this vision is how modern technology might enter into the picture. We don't normally consider what or how technology has to do with activities of souls, but for a long time I have been considering technological developments which, it turns out, very well may be exactly in that realm.

In another work I have written, **The Fusion Threshold**, which content I began developing in the early 1980's, I delved into progress being made in the technology of brain-to-computer interfaces (BCI).

> *By the time I wrote the first version of this composition, I, as a computer software developer, had been considering for several years before that point, a great dichotomy. This was the immense disparity between the advances made, over the years since computers were first developed until that time, in computer processing, storage, and transmission capabilities vs. the lack of advance in computer input through keyboards. I wondered, "What would happen if this limitation were overcome? Suppose that instead of entering information into a computer through a keyboard, a mechanism only marginally improved during the century or so since it was invented, what if we could somehow transmit information directly from our minds into computers through some kind of radio frequency link? But then further suppose that many computer users could do the same thing, and that these users were linked together through a large communications network, and that the high speed links between the computers and the users were two-way, rather than just one way?"*

As I thought about it, I formulated my own admittedly highly speculative answers to these questions. But these answers were so bizarre and seemingly out of place anywhere except in science fiction, that I felt compelled to get some shred of confirmation that my thought processes were still sane.

My researches led me to formulate predictions that have been highly accurate, and now, in late 2025, we have, as I expected, reached a point where BCI networking is on the very threshold of being able to form networks enabling people to "think" to each other, rather than "talk" to each other, in a quasi-telepathic manner. This has VERY far-reaching implications that, surprisingly, few have really considered.

The first near-term effect will be that information interchange among people will occur at far faster rates than happen at present. E.g., instead of taking all the time you spent in reading this narrative, it would take you perhaps a few seconds instead, or maybe even less. This will be due to the ***exponentially accelerating pace of cross-technology interactions*** supporting network development, and, in fact, even caused by this network development itself. Likewise, information interchange among the people on the network will be comparably accelerated.

Soon after that, the next effect will be that the data transmission speeds of the networks will facilitate not just transfer of words among its members, but also complete thoughts, visualizations, memories, and even true emotions. (I assure you that I'm not the only one contemplating this.)

Bear in mind that these interactions will occur eventually (which will be soon) among large groups of people, not just small clubs. The next effect, the one having the most profound impact, will be when the entire contents of individual's minds will be able to be uploaded to a network repository and then be merged with the knowledge of all other minds and Artificial Intelligence facilities, forming a combined Super-Mind yet still connected to all individual's brains/minds, having control over all machinery that produces everything that everyone needs.

Yes, I know. That sounds crazy. But, if you stood at Kitty Hawk, North Carolina on December 17, 1903, as the Wright brothers first flew their machine, and told the other spectators, or even the Wright brothers themselves, that within 66 years, just one lifetime, that this crude, clumsy, dangerous machine would be developed into a system capable of a round trip to the moon, would they have believed you? And again, due to the much faster pace of technology development we now enjoy, we can expect comparable BCI advancements to occur MUCH faster.

The point I'm trying to make is that the technology landscape of the world in which *Moshiach* will operate will be very different from what it is even today, and that these changes are coming VERY fast. Yet, the final effects, in terms of the morality landscape predicted by the Prophets of ancient times can yet come to pass just as they foresaw. One way that we can help effectuate this desirable result is to encourage the injection of the kind of Torah knowledge that the Prophets had into the nascent BCI network(s). ***This means <u>a requirement</u> for encouraging Torah scholars to participate in the growth of these BCI networks, in contrast to how they are discouraged from using the Internet today*** (with good reason, given the kind of morality currently prevalent on "social media" networks.) *The very last thing we want to have happen is for the Torah observant community to isolate itself from the growing BCI network community*! Their participation will be *critical* for the proper development of Free Will within the new psychologically and philosophically integrated community.

THE FINAL PLAN

What is the final outcome of all of this? I believe it will be the
fulfillment of the Final Plan that God had in mind when he
Created the universe. What could that have been?

First, we would need to understand what initial motivations
God would have had. To do that, we might want to have some
idea of Who God is and What he is like. We have been told,
however, by many scriptural sources that it is impossible to
know those things, that they are beyond human comprehension.
That makes perfect sense: we are in exactly the same position
that the *Flatland* square was in when he tried to understand
what the solid sphere was like. I.e., we should definitely
expect that we inhabitants of a four-dimensional space-time
continuum will not be able to truly understand the nature
of God residing in, what from our perspective is His higher
dimensionality. And that goes as well for other such entities, as
angels and the components of souls that connect to Heaven.

Notwithstanding that, we do have some firm beliefs about God
that are universally accepted and are consistent with the picture
of the higher-dimensionality Heaven abode for Him that we
have been in our view developing:

> 1.   God is All-Powerful, capable of doing
> absolutely anything that can possibly be done, including
> all sorts of things that we cannot imagine.

> 2.   God has absolute Free Will; He can do
> absolutely anything and everything He wants to do and
> nothing can thwart that Will.

> 3.   God desires that the results of the actions
> derived from His Free Will and the Free Will of His

Creations will promote the Good, as He defines it.

4.   Given that "Man is made in God's image", we might infer that people are some kind of projections of God's existence. But given the vast diversity in the nature of people, it's problematic to infer the nature of God from this.

That being the case, what would have motivated Him to Create the universe in the first place? The scriptures indicate that the early Prophets and commentators were convinced that God was motivated by Love for Mankind. In this context, "Love" has a very specific meaning, which in essence is the strong propensity to give something desirable to another. What would He give, and to whom would He give it?

I believe the answer to that appears in a brief passage in Torah: Deuteronomy 14:1 "*You are (the) children of Hashem, Your God*". He wanted, with His Love, to Create and give to new entities who would have a relationship with Him like the one we are capable of understanding as that of Parent to child. And to allow *us* to have that understanding, He made Mankind in such a way that they would themselves experience being parents and children.

What then was He giving? I believe He was giving Mankind a power heretofore unique to Him and absent among all other living creatures, Free Will. No other living creature actually has Free Will; they all operate under the "dictates" of their hormones and enzymes, and their inborn instincts. Mankind was going to be different. As "children of God", Mankind was going to "inherit" this essential aspect of God, Free Will.

In order for that to happen, humans had to be different from other animals from the very time of birth. All other animals, when they are born, either have some skills for survival, such as the ability to run right after being born, or they are born in very large groups which help ensure that enough of them survive to sustain the species. Also, species that live in groups are born already knowing how to form such groups and live within them in harmony with other members of the groups.

This is not the case with humans. They are born either singly or in small groups at most, and completely helpless and defenseless, and with no knowledge of how to do anything, particularly knowledge of how to live in a society. Given that their minds start out in such an empty state, they are also not encumbered by inborn instincts directing them how to behave. They can have Free Will, but it's not guaranteed that they *will* have Free Will, since they are still also born with biological "ingredients" that engender physical and emotional urges, rather in common with other animals.

Then the problem is that they will need to develop into people who can live together harmoniously in societies, which would be a main manifestation of the Good desired by God. To do that, they will need to exercise their Free Will in such a way that they will overcome urges engendered by the needs of their bodies that would otherwise thwart the ability to live harmoniously with others, and thus cause conflict.

For that to happen, parents need to raise their children, to guide them, to teach them so that they will learn to use their Free Will in such a way that they can function well in society. This, I infer, is the reason God set up this parent-child relationship pattern for humans to follow.

And for parents to know what to teach their children, how would that happen? God could directly tell parents what to teach their children, but if He did that, it would take Free Will away from the parents, who would be unable then to transmit it to their children. So, what did He do instead?

According to our scriptures, He picked a small subset of the human race and designated them as the conduit transmitting the required teachings to the rest of humanity. This group needed to have specific characteristics, in addition to being small:

> • They needed to be mobile, at least not be a stationary target for enemies, and be able to survive having to move around in exiles, which God knew would eventually occur.

> • They needed to have a penchant for literacy, to help preserve learning, in addition to having good memories and good articulation to transmit the required learning.

> • They needed to be experienced in being held in, and then liberated from, slavery so that they would well understand the difference between Freedom and Bondage.

> • They needed to be able to know they were receiving instructions from the Real God when all of them together received the instructions. In this environment, they would all need to exercise their Free Will to accept the instructions, which could happen as a consequence of their now knowing the advantage of Freedom over Bondage.

> • They needed to be stubborn and "stiff necked" as a cultural characteristic so they could resist attempts to make them abandon the instructions.

This last characteristic was a double-edged sword. On the

one hand, it enabled these people to stubbornly adhere to the instructions they were given, but on the other hand it enabled strong willed people among them to distort or resist the instructions and cause others to do the same.

This, apparently it turned out, played into God's plan to have His instructions distributed around the world, since it caused rebelliousness in these people to be punished by being scattered around the world, enabling the instructions to be widely distributed, yet also causing their stubbornness to prevent them from being absorbed into other populations. The distribution and reception of the instructions was all to be done voluntarily, thus continuing the chain of Free Will.

This people, of course, was the Nation Of Israel, and the instructions they were tasked with transmitting is the Torah, containing the information to enable people apply their Free Will to attain the Good desired by God. This body of information, both Written and Oral, was ingeniously "engineered" is such a way that even though it was impossible for it to provide guidance in all situations that might arise in a society, it provided mechanisms whereby the needed new guidance could be generated by the people themselves in congruence with previous guidance. The guidance it contains, allowing Mankind to form a harmonious society, is precisely what is also needed for the Ultimate BCI Network that is about to be formed.

The Bottom Line is that God wanted for His "children" to learn how to employ their Free Will to form harmonious societies so that they could ... what? This is where the BCI technology comes in. As described above, **through this technology we are about to achieve a situation where the totality of human consciousness will become integrated into a *single* Super-Mind** (with all souls likewise integrated within the higher dimensions along with the conscious minds), also integrated with all Artificial Intelligence controlled machines, **having the power to achieve its desires merely by exercising its Free Will and thought, reminiscent of how God makes things happen.** Also, however, **this requires the wisdom of Torah to provide guidance on how to use that combination of power and Free Will for the Good**. I.e., Humanity will, like the Children of God they were intended to be, grow up to resemble their Parent!

At that point, I suppose, God might relate to His Children rather like a Parent relates to Adult Children. What They will do, I presume, will be something consistent with dwelling in the higher dimensions of Heaven, which evidently would constitute a major component of The Next World, including The End Of Days. This, I hope, explains the Purpose behind God Creating the universe as a "playpen" for His young Children (as we are now, compared to what we will become) as they are to develop, and thus the Motivation behind that Purpose.

If all of this is any reflection of reality, then one would expect that Torah, itself, should also contain some information relevant to the scenario presented here. In fact, I believe, it does. Here is a passage that all commentators agree refers to the times of the Final Redemption:

> *DEUTERONOMY 30*
> *1 And it shall come to pass, when all these things are come upon thee, the blessing and the curse, which I have set before thee, and thou shalt bethink thyself among all the nations, whither HASHEM thy God hath driven thee, 2 and shalt return unto HASHEM thy God, and hearken to His voice according to all that I command thee this day, thou and thy children, with all thy heart,*

and with all thy soul; 3 that then HASHEM thy God will turn thy captivity, and have compassion upon thee, and will return and gather thee from all the peoples, whither HASHEM thy God hath scattered thee. 4 If any of thine that are dispersed be in the uttermost parts of heaven, from thence will HASHEM thy God gather thee, and from thence will He fetch thee. 5 And HASHEM thy God will bring thee into the land which thy fathers possessed, and thou shalt possess it; and He will do thee good, and multiply thee above thy fathers. 6 And HASHEM thy God will circumcise thy heart, and the heart of thy seed, to love HASHEM thy God with all thy heart, and with all thy soul, that thou mayest live. 7 And HASHEM thy God will put all these curses upon thine enemies, and on them that hate thee, that persecuted thee. 8 And thou shalt return and hearken to the voice of HASHEM, and do all His commandments which I command thee this day. 9 And HASHEM thy God will make thee over-abundant in all the work of thy hand, in the fruit of thy body, and in the fruit of thy cattle, and in the fruit of thy land, for good; for HASHEM will again rejoice over thee for good, as He rejoiced over thy fathers; 10 if thou shalt hearken to the voice of HASHEM thy God, to keep His commandments and His statutes which are written in this book of the law; if thou turn unto HASHEM thy God with all thy heart, and with all thy soul.

Hebrew, like many other languages, has separate singular and plural forms for the word "you". (English also used to have this with "thou" as a singular form for "you", and "ye" as a plural form, but this has gone out of usage outside of older biblical translations.) In this passage all of the occurrences of "you" and its various forms are *singular*.

In fact, in the Hebrew text of all of Deuteronomy Chapter 30, when referring to possible or actual future events, Moses uses:

- Singular "you" forms: 26 times (including pronouns, suffixes, and verbs like אַתָּה, ־ךָ, תִּשְׁמַע).

- Plural "you" forms: 5 times (including suffixes and verbs like לָכֶם, תֹּאבֵדוּן).

Virtually the entire Book of Deuteronomy is a transcript of an address that Moses gave before the entire Nation of Israel just prior to their entry into the Land of Israel. I.e., he was addressing a large crowd, many thousands of people. In such a situation, why would he use a singular form of "you" when talking to all of these people?

One reasonable explanation is that he wanted to emphasize how the things he was saying were personally relevant to each person in the audience, and this was a rhetorical device to make that point. However, if that was the case why would events he mentioned, presumably in the distant future, be *personally* relevant to anyone in the audience?

But another reasonable explanation is that Moses was prophetically anticipating that at the time of *Moshiach*, the people, in a more literal sense, *would be a singular entity*, as postulated above. Which explanation is correct? Well, now, that's up to your Free Will!

THE COMPREHENSIVE FRAMEWORK

The "comprehensive framework of thought" that I desired has assembled into place. A good starting point is Genesis 2:7 *Then the LORD God formed man of the dust of the ground, and breathed into his nostrils the breath of life; and man became a living soul.* God started with two components for the project of Creating a vessel for the soul which would support subsequent souls having Free Will: "dust of the ground", and air.

To have these two items, the planet Earth had to be formed according to a design that would provide these in the correct configurations. I.e., the Earth had to be a sphere of the correct size, mass and composition so that, among other things, it would have the correct amount of gravity so that the air would stay close to the ground and not float off into space, water would accumulate in places conducive to support of human and other life, and the ground on the surface would contain nutrients and other components to allow for development of Man and agriculture.

This meant that the Earth had to be placed in a solar system, at just the right distance from the sun so that it would receive just the right amount of energy to support life. In addition, the Earth itself had to be formed from a variety of chemical elements that came from the "outside". Outside of Earth was the total expanse of outer space.

In outer space, the source for this material was remnants of collapsed-then-exploding stars, which provided the heavier-than-helium elemental ingredients of all of the solid non-stellar bodies: planets, moons, asteroids, comets, and interstellar dust.

Before those stars were formed, a cosmically large dense cloud of hydrogen gas had to be created with enough mass that its internal gravitational attraction would cause the hydrogen to coalesce into spheres with such force as to cause the hydrogen atoms to undergo fusion into helium, thus forming stars. That initial cloud of hydrogen emerged from the Big Bang.

Science cannot come up with an explanation of what caused the Big Bang, but Torah and the concept of higher dimensions can provide a reasonable framework. As I've mentioned, my interpretation of the Creation scenario in Genesis leads me to believe that during the six "days" of Creation, the things being Created were the laws of physics, chemistry, etc. governing the existence of the universe rather than the explicit items mentioned. Along with that, we notice that the basic physical constants governing the structure and function of the universe fall within very narrow limits required to support the existence of life, as we know it, on Earth. These narrow ranges of physical constant values are commonly known as the "Goldilocks Zones". This is totally consistent with the concept that the universe was "intelligently designed" by God "for the sake of Man".

It's instructive to look at the ebb and flow empires and leaders through the panorama of history through the lens of Torah. Although science and Torah do not agree on the physical age of the universe, interestingly enough, Torah does peg the beginning of human civilization at about the same time as the beginning of recorded history. It seems to me that knowledge of Torah would enable one to anticipate the outcomes of the actions of the leaders of empires and would-be empires.

In among the events of early human history, according to Torah, were several events and situations which seem to have transcended the laws of physics. These included:

• Noah's Ark – which should not have been large enough

to contain all of the required samples of the world's animals

• Destruction of Sodom and Gomorrah – which could not have been done by any known type of explosive or natural disaster of the time

• Plagues on Egypt before the Exodus – which appeared not have natural sources

• Parting of the "Red Sea" – splitting, then reconstituting, at just the needed moments

• Sun standing still – during Joshua's battle against the Amorites (Joshua 10:12-14)

• Ark of the Covenant – not taking up space in the Temple.

It's highly conceivable that all of these could have been manifestations of a manipulation of space-time, potentially tied to higher-dimensional phenomena, as they are consistent with the possibility of such manipulation.

Along the path of history, it seems that God reached a point like a parent bird that needs to push its offspring out of the nest to force them to learn to fly. At that point, principally around the destruction of the Second Temple, He stopped routine communication with people through prophecy, and essentially remained "hidden". Now, His children were much more "on their own", needing to rely on Torah for properly developing their Free Will, like children old enough not to need parents "looking over their shoulders" for their development.

Fast forward to the present. As I mentioned, the exponentially accelerating pace of *cross-technology interactions* is fueling the situation whereby technological developments are occurring with such dazzling frequency that we are fast approaching what is commonly called the Singularity. In case you are not familiar with that mathematical term, it refers to growth, in this case that of technological development frequency, due to exponential increase of same, which is approaching a point analogous to that being reached by dividing any non-zero number by another one that is approaching zero. Graphically, that looks like this:

In our case, the Singularity essentially will be reached when the totality of human consciousness becomes integrated into the single Super-Mind, enabling the component minds to develop interacting technologies *in effectively no extents of time*. This will result in new technological developments occurring at a pace *orders of magnitude faster* than currently. And shepherding that process will, I expect, be one of the main tasks of *Moshiach*. [Some common usage of "Singularity" refers to a point when Artificial Intelligence reaches and passes human intelligence. This is not the true meaning of the word.]

Of course, it's purely speculation as to what will happen next, but within the framework of coherence I've built for understanding all of the information I've seen, both within Torah and history, I expect that all of the ancient prophecies about *Moshiach* and The End Of Days will come to pass.

One of *Moshiach*'s tasks, according to these prophecies, is the worldwide elimination of Evil. It's outside the awareness of most people that the primary source of Evil in this world is that fact *the consciousness of each human is totally separate from that of each other human*. This separation, of course, enables people to conceal information from each other, and this concealment capability allows people to keep truths that they know secret, and then deceive one another. This separation is the source of all lies, "disinformation", and misrepresentation, i.e., a major source of Evil. Another source of Evil is the hostile psychological wall each person's ego can put up against anyone else's. This prompts people to physically act against each other with violence. These sources of Evil are outside of most people's awareness because that has always been the nature of humans ever since humanity began, and continues to be so now.

As I note above, this is about to change. When we reach the Singularity, this separation of consciousness will disappear! As I stated in ***The Fusion Threshold***:

> Now we come to the very crux of the matter. What is it that truly differentiates you from me or from anyone else? To be more specific, when we each say the pronoun 'I', what is the difference between what you are talking about, and what I am talking about? Today, the fact that we have two separate physical bodies, aside from anything else, would suffice. No matter what we would like to do, we are destined from birth to become separate,

and separated, persons. You grow, learn, and gather your experiences, and I gather mine. They cannot be the same. We are never in the exactly the same place at the same time, although if we both watch the same TV program at the same, the experience, albeit limited only to narrow sight and sound, comes close. Even so, our eyes, ears, and brains are not precisely the same. Particularly our brains: we selectively limit our perceptions. There are many well known psychological experiments, beloved by defense attorneys, which show that several eyewitnesses of an event will generally report significantly different versions of what they saw, and most will be wrong.

So, we are differentiated by the fact that our bodies and brains are physically different, and our brains contain differing sets of information relating to knowledge and experience. On top of that, the means of communication to allow us to exchange knowledge and experience are woefully inadequate. We depend on spoken and written language, and a limited amount of visual or graphic presentation to exchange knowledge. These are just as likely to contribute to misunderstanding as to communication, and are actually the basis for most problems in the world among people. That is, we fail to properly understand one another due to improper communication, and when we do understand, we must do it too slowly for it to do as much good as it could. ...

In order to appreciate fully the magnitude of change that society will undergo, it must be understood that the separateness of individual people, such as it has always been throughout our history, is the fundamental fact of life underlying all of our social institutions. Our governments, families, employment situations, schools, recreational activities, and social groups are all constituted the way we find them now because of the separateness of their members. The pecking orders, the political squabbles, the status symbols, the schools of hard knocks: these are all the result of never being sure what is going on in the other person's head. How could it be otherwise? ... It's this innate inability to communicate across the separation between individuals that has always caused our inability to form overall successful social and political groupings on a global scale that I mentioned earlier.

But, what will happen in the new environment? What will happen when you can have access to all the information you need and desire about anything that is known to anyone, and so can everyone else? What will happen when you can make your thoughts completely, correctly, and quickly understood by all others, and they can make theirs likewise understood to you? What will happen when you have total access to the world's resources to fulfill your needs and desires, and there is no longer any need to compete for such fulfillment? What will happen when disease, aging, and death no longer look over your shoulder and breathe down your neck?

You will be able to know everything that everyone else knows, and everyone else will be able to know everything that you know.

In such an environment, there will be no such thing as secrets; there will be no possibility or even desire to deceive anyone, or have conflict against anyone else. There will be no lying or hostility; these sources of Evil will disappear!

I am well aware that most people who are exposed to these ideas are, to one extent or another, repulsed by them. They realize that it means that the concepts like Privacy and Autonomy will disappear, and they hold these "possessions" to be precious values, like Liberty. Yes, Privacy and Autonomy will become obsolete, just as horse-dependent transportation became obsolete when the automobile became available.

It will be as if you could physically separate many parts of your body from each other yet have all of them work harmoniously together while fully controlled by your brain. You would have a single consciousness; there would just be a single "you". Your separated parts would have no use or concept of Privacy, since no part would have any "private" or proprietary information; they would all share your consciousness. The only difference now will be that instead of your mind controlling a body of integrated parts, as it does now, or separated body parts as discussed, it will instead control separated full people, but their minds will be integrated, i.e., yours combined with everyone else's. (Being "Of One Mind" will take on a whole new *LITERAL* meaning!)

I imagine that acceptance of this situation will vary inversely with people's ages, i.e., younger people will be more receptive. Even today, we see that younger people embrace "social media" and are willing to expose personal information there rather more than their elders, often to the younger people's detriment, due to others in these systems employing deceptive practices (as noted above).

But if *Moshiach* can manage the development of this BCI Super-Mind system with appropriate Torah guidance, which the prophecies say he will, then this can be the mechanism by which the highly desirable results of his actions will all come to pass.

And part of that will be the bridging of Earth-bound

consciousness with the soul's component in higher dimensional Heaven, enabling Man to truly know God, and exercise Free Will as He intended.

And truly understanding all of that leaves us in the same position as the square trying to understand the nature of the sphere.

APPENDIX

From X.com-Grok AI:

Brain-Computer Interfaces And Higher Dimensions

The idea of brain-computer interfaces (BCIs) connecting to higher-dimensional space is speculative and rooted in theoretical physics, neuroscience, and philosophy. While no established scientific theory directly links BCIs to higher-dimensional spaces, several concepts and hypotheses provide a framework for exploring this possibility.

1. Information Theory and Consciousness in Higher Dimensions

- Context: Some theories suggest consciousness might interact with or emerge from higher-dimensional structures beyond the three spatial dimensions we perceive. For instance, certain interpretations of string theory or M-theory propose that reality includes additional spatial dimensions (up to 10 or 11 in some models) that are compactified or inaccessible to our senses.

- Connection to BCIs: BCIs, which interface neural activity with computational systems, could theoretically tap into or simulate processes that align with higher-dimensional information processing. For example:

  - Neural Encoding of Higher Dimensions: The brain's neural networks might encode information in ways that resemble higher-dimensional topologies (e.g., neural manifolds). BCIs could amplify or externalize this encoding, potentially allowing interaction with abstract higher-dimensional spaces.

- Quantum Consciousness Hypotheses: Theories like the Orch-OR (Orchestrated Objective Reduction) model by Penrose and Hameroff suggest consciousness involves quantum processes in microtubules. If these processes interact with higher-dimensional quantum fields, BCIs might indirectly access such realms by decoding quantum-like neural signals.

- Speculative Leap: A sufficiently advanced BCI could act as a bridge, translating neural patterns into a computational framework that mimics or interfaces with higher-dimensional information structures, though this remains highly theoretical.

2. Holographic Principle and Neural Interfaces

- Context: The holographic principle, derived from string theory and black hole physics, posits that all information within a volume of space can be encoded on a lower-dimensional boundary. For example, a 3D universe could be a projection of information encoded on a 2D surface.

- Connection to BCIs: The brain might process information in a way analogous to a holographic system, where complex perceptions are encoded in lower-dimensional neural structures. BCIs could theoretically "read" or project these encodings into external systems, potentially mimicking access to higher-dimensional data structures.

- Speculative Leap: If the universe itself is a hologram with higher-dimensional underpinnings, BCIs might enable humans to interface with or manipulate the boundary conditions of this hologram, effectively interacting with higher-dimensional information.

3. BCIs and Simulation Hypothesis

- Context: The simulation hypothesis, popularized by Nick Bostrom, suggests we might live in a simulated reality. Higher-dimensional spaces could be the "hardware" or framework running the simulation, existing outside our perceived 3D reality.

- Connection to BCIs: Advanced BCIs could theoretically interface with the underlying code of the simulation. For instance:

  - Neural interfaces might detect or manipulate signals that correspond to the simulation's higher-dimensional framework.

  - BCIs could allow users to "hack" or perceive aspects of the simulation's architecture, which might exist in higher-dimensional computational spaces.

- Speculative Leap: A BCI with sufficient resolution could bridge human consciousness to the higher-dimensional "source code" of reality, allowing interaction with or perception of dimensions beyond our sensory experience.

4. Non-Local Consciousness and BCIs

- Context: Some fringe theories, like those in parapsychology or panpsychism, propose that consciousness is non-local, existing in or interacting with higher-dimensional or non-physical realms. For example, theories of a "quantum mind" suggest consciousness might transcend classical spacetime.

- Connection to BCIs: BCIs could theoretically amplify or detect non-local signals if consciousness indeed interacts with higher-dimensional spaces. For instance:

  - BCIs might pick up on subtle neural correlates of non-local phenomena, such as entanglement-like effects in brain activity.

  - Advanced BCIs could interface with hypothetical fields (e.g., a consciousness field) that exist in higher-dimensional frameworks.

- Speculative Leap: If consciousness is fundamentally tied to higher-dimensional spaces, BCIs might serve as tools to access or manipulate these realms, though this lacks empirical support.

5. Mathematical and Computational Models

- Context: Higher-dimensional spaces are often studied in mathematics and physics (e.g., Kaluza-Klein theory, which unifies gravity and electromagnetism in five dimensions). Computational models of neural networks sometimes use higher-dimensional mathematics to describe complex brain dynamics.

- Connection to BCIs: BCIs rely on decoding high-dimensional neural data (e.g., firing patterns across thousands of neurons). This data can be represented in abstract mathematical spaces with many dimensions.

  - Advanced BCIs could use dimensionality reduction or expansion techniques to map neural activity onto higher-dimensional computational spaces, potentially simulating interactions with higher-dimensional structures.

  - Machine learning models in BCIs might inadvertently mimic higher-dimensional processing, aligning with theoretical physics models of reality.

- Speculative Leap: If the brain's information processing inherently reflects higher-dimensional structures, BCIs could act as translators, allowing humans to perceive or interact with these dimensions through computational interfaces.

Current Limitations and Speculation

- Scientific Gaps: No direct evidence links BCIs to higher-dimensional spaces. Most connections are speculative, relying on unproven theories about consciousness, quantum mechanics, or the nature of reality.

- Technological Constraints: Current BCIs (e.g., Neuralink, BrainGate) focus on practical applications like motor control or communication, not metaphysical exploration. They lack the resolution or theoretical grounding to access higher-dimensional phenomena.

- Philosophical Considerations: The idea hinges on untested assumptions about consciousness and reality. Higher-dimensional spaces, as described in physics, are typically compactified or inaccessible, making direct interaction unlikely with current technology.

Conclusion

Theories connecting BCIs to higher-dimensional spaces are speculative and draw from interdisciplinary ideas: information theory, quantum consciousness, the holographic principle, simulation hypothesis, and non-local consciousness. While BCIs could theoretically interface with complex neural patterns or computational models that mimic higher-dimensional structures, no empirical evidence supports direct interaction with higher-dimensional spaces. Future advances in neuroscience, physics, and BCI technology might provide new insights, but for now, these connections remain in the realm of theoretical exploration.

The Nature Of Heaven In Tanach

In the Tanach (the Hebrew Bible), the concept of "Heaven" is multifaceted, serving as both a physical and spiritual concept, though it differs significantly from later Christian or Western notions of Heaven as a distinct afterlife destination. The Hebrew term most commonly associated with Heaven is *shamayim* (שָׁמַיִם), which appears frequently and carries various meanings depending on context. Below is an exploration of the nature of Heaven as referenced in the Tanach:

1. Heaven as the Physical Sky or Cosmos

- Description: The most common use of *shamayim* refers to the physical heavens— the sky, atmosphere, or celestial realm where stars, sun, and moon reside. It is part of the created order, distinct from Earth.

- Key Examples:

  - Genesis 1:1: "In the beginning, God created the heavens (*shamayim*) and the earth." Here, *shamayim* refers to the sky or cosmos as part of creation.

  - Genesis 1:8: God calls the firmament (a dome-like structure separating waters) *shamayim*, indicating the sky.

  - Psalm 19:1: "The heavens declare the glory of God; the skies proclaim the work of His hands." The heavens are a testament to God's creative power.

- Nature: This is a physical, observable realm, not necessarily a spiritual afterlife. It includes the atmosphere (where birds fly, e.g., Genesis 1:20) and the starry expanse (e.g., Genesis 15:5).

2. Heaven as God's Dwelling Place

- Description: The Tanach often depicts Heaven as the abode of God, a spiritual or transcendent realm where God resides and rules. It is less a place of human souls and more a symbol of divine presence and authority. [A notable exception to this is DEUTERONOMY 30:4 *If any of thine that are dispersed be in the uttermost parts of Heaven, from thence will the LORD thy God gather thee, and from thence will He fetch thee.* This clearly indicates that the "dispersed" people might at some point dwell in Heaven.]

- Key Examples:

  - Deuteronomy 26:15: "Look down from Your holy habitation, from heaven (*shamayim*), and bless Your people Israel." Heaven is where God "resides" in a metaphorical sense.

  - Isaiah 6:1-3: Isaiah's vision of God on a throne with *seraphim* (a type of angel) suggests a heavenly court, a divine realm beyond human access.

  - Psalm 11:4: "The Lord is in His holy temple; the Lord's throne is in heaven (*shamayim*)."

- Nature: Heaven is a spiritual domain associated with God's sovereignty, not explicitly a destination for human souls. It is often described symbolically (e.g., with thrones or angels) to convey God's transcendence.

3. Heaven as a Symbol of Divine Power or Blessing

- Description: Heaven is frequently referenced as the source of God's actions, blessings, or judgments, emphasizing its role as the seat of divine authority.

- Key Examples:

  - Genesis 7:11: During the Flood, "the windows of the heavens (*shamayim*) were opened," symbolizing divine control over natural forces.

  - Deuteronomy 11:11: The land of Israel drinks water "from the rain of heaven," indicating God's provision.

  - 1 Kings 8:35: Solomon prays for God to hear from Heaven and forgive, linking Heaven to divine response.

- Nature: Heaven represents God's active presence in the world, often tied to natural phenomena (rain, fire) or divine intervention.

4. Absence of Heaven as an Afterlife Destination

- Description: Unlike later Jewish, Christian, or Islamic traditions, the Tanach rarely, if ever, describes Heaven as a place where human souls go after death. The afterlife in the Tanach is more commonly associated with *Sheol*, a shadowy underworld for all souls, righteous or wicked (e.g., Ecclesiastes 9:10, Psalm 6:5).

- Key Examples:

  - Genesis 5:24: Enoch "walked with God, and he was not, for God took him," which some interpret as an ascension to Heaven, though the text is vague.

  - 2 Kings 2:11: Elijah is taken up to Heaven in a whirlwind, a rare instance of a human entering the divine realm, but this is exceptional and not a general promise.

- Nature: The Tanach focuses on earthly life and covenant with God, with little emphasis on a heavenly afterlife. Any suggestion of humans in Heaven (e.g., Enoch, Elijah) is ambiguous and not a developed doctrine.

5. Heaven in Poetic and Prophetic Contexts

- Description: In poetic and prophetic books, Heaven is often used metaphorically or symbolically to convey God's majesty, judgment, or cosmic order.

- Key Examples:

  - Isaiah 66:1: "Heaven is My throne, and the earth is My footstool," emphasizing God's universal sovereignty.

  - Amos 9:6: "He who builds His upper chambers in the heavens (*shamayim*)" portrays God as the cosmic architect.

  - Nature: These references use Heaven to elevate God's status above creation, not to describe a literal place for human souls.

Key Characteristics of Heaven in the Tanach:

- Physical and Spiritual: Heaven is both the visible sky (cosmos) and the invisible dwelling of God, blending material and transcendent meanings.

- God-Centered: It is primarily the realm of God's presence, throne, and activity, not a human destination.

- Symbolic: Heaven often symbolizes divine power, order, or intervention, especially in poetic or prophetic texts.

- Limited Afterlife Role: The Tanach does not develop Heaven as a paradise for souls, focusing instead on earthly covenant and *Sheol* for the dead.

Notes:

- The concept of Heaven as a paradise for the righteous emerges more clearly in later Second Temple Judaism (e.g., in texts like 1 Enoch or the Dead Sea Scrolls) and is influenced by Hellenistic and Persian ideas, but these are outside the Tanach.

In Rabbinic Judaism, the concept of Heaven—often referred to as Gan Eden (Garden of Eden), *Olam HaBa* (the World to Come), or *Shamayim* (the Heavens)—is elaborated upon extensively in sources outside the Tanach (Hebrew Bible), particularly in the Talmud, Midrash, and later Rabbinic texts like the Zohar and medieval commentaries. These sources provide a richer, more detailed picture of Heaven compared to the relatively sparse references in the Tanach. Below is an overview of the nature of Heaven as described in these

Rabbinic sources, focusing on its characteristics, purpose, and spiritual significance:

1. Heaven as Gan Eden (The Garden of Eden)

- Description: Gan Eden is often depicted as a spiritual paradise where righteous souls reside after death. It is distinct from the physical Garden of Eden in Genesis, serving as a celestial realm of reward.

- Nature:

  - A place of spiritual bliss where souls experience closeness to God (the Divine Presence, or *Shechinah*).

  - Described as a realm of intellectual and spiritual delight, where the righteous "bask in the radiance of the Divine Presence" (Talmud, Berachot 17a).

  - Some sources portray Gan Eden as having multiple levels or compartments, accommodating souls based on their merit (Midrash Rabbah, Genesis 14:5).

- Purpose: A reward for the righteous, where they enjoy eternal spiritual fulfillment, free from physical suffering or material concerns.

- Source: Talmud (Shabbat 152b), Midrash Tanhuma, and Zohar (e.g., Zohar I:4b).

2. Heaven as *Olam HaBa* (The World to Come)

- Description: *Olam HaBa* is often distinguished

from Gan Eden in Rabbinic literature, referring to a future eschatological era or a post-resurrection spiritual reality, though the terms are sometimes used interchangeably.

- Nature:

  - A state of ultimate spiritual perfection, where souls are reunited with resurrected bodies after the Messianic era (Talmud, Sanhedrin 90b-92a).

  - Unlike Gan Eden, which may be an interim state for souls, *Olam HaBa* is eternal and tied to the ultimate redemption of humanity.

  - Descriptions emphasize intellectual and spiritual rewards, such as studying Torah with God or experiencing divine wisdom (Talmud, Berachot 64a).

  - Some texts suggest no physical needs (e.g., eating or drinking) exist in *Olam HaBa*, as it is purely spiritual (Talmud, Berachot 17a).

- Purpose: The ultimate destination for the righteous, fulfilling God's promise of eternal life and divine connection.

- Source: Mishnah Sanhedrin 10:1, Talmud (Rosh Hashanah 17a), and Maimonides' Mishneh Torah (Hilchot Teshuva 8:2).

3. Mystical Perspectives (Kabbalah and Zohar)

- Description: In Kabbalistic texts, Heaven is often

described in metaphysical terms, with Gan Eden and *Olam HaBa* representing different spiritual realms or states of divine consciousness.

- Nature:

  - Gan Eden is divided into Lower Gan Eden (for souls still needing purification) and Upper Gan Eden (for fully righteous souls closer to God) (Zohar I:41a).

  - Heaven is a realm where souls ascend through various spiritual levels, drawing closer to the *Ein Sof* (God's infinite essence).

  - The Zohar describes vivid imagery, such as souls being clothed in spiritual garments of light, engaging in divine contemplation, or being guided by angels (Zohar II:210b).

  - Some Kabbalistic views suggest souls merge or commune with the divine light, partially aligning with the idea of collective spiritual unity, though individuality is often retained.

- Purpose: A place for souls to refine themselves, experience divine unity, and prepare for ultimate reintegration into the divine plan.

- Source: Zohar, Sefer HaBahir, and later Kabbalistic works like those of Rabbi Isaac Luria.

4. Levels and Compartments of Heaven

- Description: Rabbinic sources frequently describe

Heaven as having multiple levels or chambers, reflecting the varying degrees of righteousness among souls.

- Nature:

  - The Talmud mentions "seven heavens" (Chagigah 12b), each with a specific spiritual function, with the highest (*Aravot*) being the abode of God's throne and the righteous souls.

  - Souls may ascend through these levels based on their deeds, Torah study, or spiritual purity (Midrash Tehillim 11:6).

  - The righteous are said to sit in divine academies (yeshivot), studying Torah with angels or biblical figures like Moses (Talmud, Ketubot 77b).

- Purpose: To accommodate the diversity of human merit, ensuring each soul receives a just reward tailored to its spiritual achievements.

- Source: Talmud (Chagigah 12b-13a), Midrash Rabbah, and Maimonides' Guide for the Perplexed (3:51).

5. Interim Role and Purification

- Description: Some souls may require purification before entering Gan Eden or *Olam HaBa*, often in a transitional realm like *Gehinnom* (a purgatory-like state) or Lower Gan Eden.

- Nature:

- *Gehinnom* is not eternal for most souls but serves to cleanse sins, after which souls ascend to Heaven (Talmud, Eruvin 19a).

- The process is temporary, typically lasting no more than 12 months, except for the most wicked (Mishnah Eduyot 2:10).

- Heaven, in contrast, is the eternal reward for those who have been purified or were righteous in life.

- Purpose: To prepare souls for eternal communion with God by removing spiritual impurities.

- Source: Talmud (Shabbat 33b), Zohar (III:220b), and Ramban's Sha'ar HaGemul.

6. Key Characteristics Across Sources

- Spiritual Over Physical: Heaven is primarily a spiritual realm, with physical descriptions (e.g., banquets, rivers of light) often interpreted as metaphors for spiritual joy (Maimonides, Mishneh Torah, Hilchot Teshuva 8:2).

- Closeness to God: The ultimate reward is experiencing the Divine Presence, described as the greatest pleasure (Talmud, Berachot 17a).

- Individuality vs. Unity: While some Kabbalistic texts hint at a partial merging of souls into divine unity, most Rabbinic sources emphasize that souls retain individuality to experience personal reward (Zohar I:66a; Ramban's writings).

- Dynamic Process: Heaven is not static; souls may ascend through levels, engage in spiritual growth, or participate in divine activities like Torah study.

Notes:

- While Rabbinic sources don't typically describe souls "merging together" in the collective sense of some philosophies (e.g., non-dualism or panpsychism), Kabbalistic texts like the Zohar occasionally suggest a mystical unity where souls connect with the divine essence, though they retain distinct identities. This differs from complete merging, as individuality is preserved for reward and relationship with God.

- Sources: Key texts include the Babylonian Talmud (e.g., Berachot, Sanhedrin, Chagigah), Midrash Rabbah, Zohar, and commentaries by Maimonides (Mishneh Torah, Guide for the Perplexed), Ramban (Sha'ar HaGemul), and later Kabbalists like the Ari (Rabbi Isaac Luria).

- Limitations: Rabbinic descriptions of Heaven are often metaphorical or deliberately vague, as the true nature of the afterlife is considered beyond human comprehension (Talmud, Berachot 17a). Maimonides, for example, warns against overly literal interpretations.

Explanations Of The Existence Of The Universe Without Creation By God

Explaining the existence of the universe without invoking a deity involves scientific, philosophical, and speculative theories grounded in naturalistic frameworks. Here are the primary explanations:

1. Big Bang Theory:

- Overview: The universe began approximately 13.8 billion years ago from an extremely hot, dense state, expanding rapidly in an event called the Big Bang.

- Explanation: The Big Bang describes the universe's origin as a singularity—a point of infinite density and temperature. Quantum fluctuations in this singularity may have triggered the expansion. The theory doesn't address what caused the singularity but focuses on the evolution of the universe from that point.

- Evidence: Cosmic microwave background radiation, redshift of galaxies, and the abundance of light elements (e.g., hydrogen, helium).

- Source: Developed by Georges Lemaître and supported by observations from the Planck satellite and Hubble Space Telescope.

2. Quantum Cosmology:

- Overview: Quantum mechanics suggests the universe could arise from quantum fluctuations in a vacuum, where "nothing" is unstable and particles can spontaneously appear.

- Explanation: In models like those proposed by Stephen Hawking and Lawrence Krauss, the universe could emerge from a quantum vacuum state due to the uncertainty principle. The total energy of the universe may be zero (balancing positive and negative energy), allowing it to arise without an external cause.

- Key Idea: "Nothing" in quantum terms isn't truly empty but a field of potential, enabling spontaneous universe creation.

- Source: Krauss's A Universe from Nothing and Hawking's The Grand Design.

3 Multiverse Hypothesis:

- Overview: The universe may be one of many in a multiverse, where different universes have different physical constants and laws.

- Explanation: Our universe's existence could be a statistical outcome within an infinite or vast ensemble of universes. Inflationary cosmology (e.g., eternal inflation by Andrei Linde) suggests that quantum fluctuations during rapid expansion create "bubble" universes, one of which is ours.

- Key Idea: The question of "why" our universe exists is sidestepped; it's one of many, and we observe this one because it supports life (anthropic principle).

- Source: Works by Linde, Alan Guth, and Max Tegmark.

4. Cyclic Models:

- Overview: Some theories propose the universe undergoes cycles of expansion and contraction (e.g., Big Bang followed by a Big Crunch).

- Explanation: In models like the ekpyrotic universe or conformal cyclic cosmology (Roger Penrose), the universe's existence is perpetual, with no ultimate beginning. Each cycle resets the universe, avoiding the need for an initial cause.

- Key Idea: The universe is eternal, with our Big Bang being one event in an infinite series.

- Source: Penrose's Cycles of Time and Steinhardt-Turok's ekpyrotic model.

5. Philosophical Naturalism:

- Overview: Philosophers like David Hume and modern naturalists argue that the universe's existence might not require an explanation beyond itself.

- Explanation: The universe could be a "brute fact"—it exists because it exists. Asking "why" assumes a need for a cause, but the universe might be self-contained, with its laws and structure being sufficient. Alternatively, causality may only apply within the universe, not to its existence as a whole.

- Key Idea: The question of "why" may be a human construct, and the universe's existence needs no external justification.

- Source: Hume's Dialogues Concerning Natural Religion and contemporary works by philosophers like Graham Oppy.

6. String Theory and M-Theory:

- Overview: String theory posits that the universe is made of vibrating strings in higher dimensions, with M-theory unifying these ideas.

- Explanation: The universe's existence could result from interactions in higher-dimensional spaces or branes (membranes) colliding in a multiverse framework. These collisions could trigger Big Bang-like events.

- Key Idea: The universe emerges from fundamental physical processes in a higher-dimensional reality.

- Source: Works by Brian Greene (The Elegant Universe) and Edward Witten.

Notes:

- These explanations rely on empirical evidence, mathematical models, or philosophical reasoning, avoiding supernatural causes.

- None definitively answer "why" the universe exists, as science describes mechanisms rather than ultimate purposes. Philosophical naturalism often frames the question itself as potentially unanswerable or unnecessary.

Quantum Nature Of Time

The idea of a quantum nature to time stems from attempts to reconcile quantum mechanics with gravity, particularly in the context of quantum gravity theories like loop quantum gravity or string theory:

1. Time in Quantum Mechanics: In standard quantum mechanics, time is treated as a classical, continuous parameter, not a quantum observable. It's a background framework, not something that can be quantized or have superpositions like position or energy.

2. Quantum Gravity and Time: Theories of quantum gravity suggest that spacetime, including time, may have a discrete or quantized structure at the Planck scale (around 10^{-43} seconds). In loop quantum gravity, for instance, spacetime is made of tiny, discrete loops, implying that time might not flow smoothly but in tiny, indivisible "ticks."

3. Uncertainty and Time: Some interpretations propose that time could exhibit quantum-like properties, such as uncertainty. For example, in certain models, the precise measurement of time might be limited by a fundamental uncertainty related to the Planck time, analogous to the Heisenberg uncertainty principle for position and momentum.

4. Emergent Time: In some quantum gravity frameworks, time is not fundamental but emergent, arising from the interactions of quantum states. For instance, in the Wheeler-DeWitt equation, the universe's wavefunction lacks a time variable, suggesting time might emerge from correlations between quantum systems rather than existing independently.

5. Entanglement and Time: Recent research explores time's quantum nature through entanglement. Some physicists propose that time's flow could be linked to the growth of quantum entanglement between systems, like in a "clock" system entangled with the rest of the universe.

6. Experimental Hints: While there's no direct evidence for time's quantum nature, experiments probing ultra-short timescales (e.g., attosecond physics) or gravitational effects in quantum systems (e.g., quantum clocks near black holes) might eventually reveal deviations from classical time.

The quantum nature of time is still speculative, as we lack a complete theory of quantum gravity. Current models suggest time could be discrete, emergent, or tied to quantum phenomena like entanglement, but these ideas remain theoretical, with ongoing research aiming to test them.

The Concept Of God Accessing All Of History Simultaneously

In Jewish thought, the concept of God's omniscience and sovereignty over history is deeply rooted in biblical, rabbinic, and philosophical sources. These texts often emphasize God's ability to perceive all of time simultaneously and exert control over historical events. Below are key Judaic sources that address this idea:

Biblical Sources

1. Isaiah 46:9-10

   • "I am God, and there is none like Me, declaring the end from the beginning, and from ancient times things that are not yet done, saying, 'My counsel shall stand, and I will do all My pleasure.'"

   • This verse explicitly states that God knows the future from the beginning, implying a perspective that encompasses all of history at once. His ability to "declare the end from the beginning" suggests a transcendent view of time and complete control over historical outcomes.

2. Psalms 33:11

   • "The counsel of the Lord stands forever, the thoughts of His heart to all generations."

   • This highlights God's eternal plan, which remains unchanging across all generations, suggesting His mastery over the entirety of history.

3. Ecclesiastes 3:11

- "He has made everything beautiful in its time; also, He has put eternity into man's heart, yet so that he cannot find out what God has done from the beginning to the end."

- This verse implies that God operates on a level where He perceives and orchestrates all of time, while humans are limited in their ability to comprehend this scope.

4. Exodus 3:14

- "And God said to Moses, 'I AM THAT I AM.'"

- The divine name Ehyeh Asher Ehyeh (I AM THAT I AM) is interpreted by some Jewish scholars (e.g., Rashi and later philosophers) as indicating God's eternal presence, existing outside of time and thus able to perceive and control all moments simultaneously.

Rabbinic Sources

1. Pirkei Avot (Ethics of the Fathers) 2:1

- "Know what is above you: an eye that sees, an ear that hears, and all your deeds are recorded in a book."

- This teaching from the Mishnah suggests God's constant awareness of all human actions across time, implying a divine perspective that transcends temporal limitations.

2. Talmud, Berakhot 58a

- The Talmud discusses God's omniscience, with
statements like, "The Holy One, blessed be He, sees
the ways of all men." This reinforces the idea that
God's perception encompasses all events and actions
simultaneously.

3. Midrash Rabbah, Genesis 9:3

- The Midrash describes God as "the One who sees
the end at the beginning," emphasizing His ability to
perceive the entirety of history in a single moment,
aligning with His sovereignty over time and events.

Jewish Philosophical Sources

1. Maimonides (Rambam), Guide for the Perplexed (Part I,
Chapter 54)

- Maimonides argues that God's knowledge is not
bound by time, as human knowledge is. He writes
that God's omniscience encompasses all events—
past, present, and future—simultaneously, without
being limited by the sequential nature of time. This is
because God's essence is eternal and unchanging.

2. Saadia Gaon, The Book of Beliefs and Opinions (Treatise
II)

- Saadia Gaon explains that God's knowledge is
infinite and includes all events across time. He asserts
that God's foreknowledge does not negate free will
but reflects His ability to perceive all moments as
one.

3. Nachmanides (Ramban), Commentary on Genesis 1:1

- Nachmanides discusses God's transcendence over time, noting that the act of creation itself implies God's control over the entire continuum of history. He suggests that God's will sustains and directs all events from creation to the end of time.

Kabbalistic Sources

1. Zohar, Parashat Terumah 2:135b

- The Zohar, a foundational kabbalistic text, describes God as existing beyond time, with all moments of history unified in His divine perception. It uses mystical language to convey that God's "vision" encompasses all of existence in a single, eternal moment.

2. Rabbi Isaac Luria (Ari), Etz Chaim

- Lurianic Kabbalah teaches that God's infinite nature allows Him to perceive and orchestrate all events in history as part of a unified divine plan. The concept of tzimtzum (divine contraction) still allows for God's overarching control and awareness of all time.

Summary

The idea that God sees and controls all of history simultaneously is supported across Jewish texts:

- Biblical: Verses like Isaiah 46:9-10 and Psalms 33:11 emphasize God's eternal knowledge and sovereignty.

APPENDIX

- Rabbinic: Pirkei Avot and Talmudic passages highlight God's all-seeing nature and eternal record of events.

- Philosophical: Maimonides and Saadia Gaon articulate God's transcendence over time, with His knowledge encompassing all moments.

- Kabbalistic: The Zohar and Lurianic teachings describe God's perception as unifying all of history in a single divine moment.

These sources collectively affirm that God's omniscience and control extend beyond human temporal constraints, allowing Him to perceive and direct all of history as a unified whole.

Overview of Computer-Aided Telepathy

Computer-aided telepathy refers to technologies that enable direct brain-to-brain or brain-to-computer communication by decoding neural signals into actionable outputs like text, speech, or commands. Rooted in brain-computer interfaces (BCIs), it bridges neuroscience, AI, and hardware to translate thoughts without physical input. As of 2025, this field is transitioning from experimental prototypes to practical applications, primarily for medical use, with rapid advancements in accuracy, speed, and non-invasiveness. While true "mind-reading" remains limited to structured thoughts (e.g., imagined speech), recent breakthroughs suggest broader adoption within 5–10 years.

Key Advancements in 2025

- Neuralink's Telepathy Implant: Neuralink's flagship BCI, the N1 implant, has been implanted in at least seven patients worldwide, focusing on paralysis and ALS. It uses 1,024 electrodes on 64 ultrathin threads to record neural activity from the motor cortex, translating thoughts into cursor control, typing, and robotic manipulation at speeds up to 100+ words per minute. In summer 2025 updates, users like Noland Arbaugh demonstrated real-time control of computers for language study and math, while Alex controlled a Tesla Optimus robot hand for rock-paper-scissors. Canadian trials (August–September 2025) expanded to cervical spinal cord injuries, with all patients reporting stable performance and no major complications. Neuralink filed trademarks for "Telepathy" (brain-to-computer communication) and "Telekinesis" (mind-controlled devices) in March 2025, hinting at future human-to-human links.

- Non-Invasive Wearables and AI Decoders: AlterEgo's headset, unveiled in September 2025, detects sub-vocal muscle signals (silent "speech") via surface sensors, decoding them into text or commands at thought speed (up to 150 words per minute) using AI. It enables silent conversations, device control, and real-time translation, with bone-conduction audio for responses. This "near-telepathic" device is discreet and battery-efficient, targeting everyday use beyond medical needs. Separately, AI-based BCIs from Meta and UCLA achieved 80% accuracy in real-time thought-to-text decoding using EEG caps, while a Cell study reported 74% accuracy for inner speech transcription, activated by mental "passwords" for privacy.

- Speech and Intonation Restoration: A Nature Neuroscience study (July 2025) enabled a paralyzed woman to generate speech from thoughts in 3 seconds, using her pre-stroke voice from wedding videos for personalization. Another Nature paper (June 2025) hit 10-millisecond latency for intonated speech (e.g., questions, singing) at 40–60 words per minute with 60% word accuracy. These use AI to map brain signals to phonemes, marking steps toward fluid, expressive "telepathic" output.

- Emerging Research and Competitors:

  - Precision Neuroscience's surface cortical interface aims for commercial release by late 2025, focusing on minimally invasive implants for broader access.

  - NeuroXess reported Chinese speech decoding and AI conversations via BCI in January 2025.

- OpenBCI's Galea headset integrates BCI with VR for neuroscience research.

Technology	Type	Key 2025 Milestone	Accuracy/ Speed	Primary Use
Neuralink Telepathy	Invasive Implant	human 7+ implants; robot control	WPM 100+ typing	Paralysis/ALS communication
AlterEgo Headset	Non-Invasive Wearable	Silent thought-to-text demo	WPM 150	Everyday silent comms
Meta/UCLA EEG De-coder	Non-Invasive Cap	Real-time thought-to-text	accuracy 80%	General mind-reading
Nature Speech BCI	Invasive	10ms intonated speech	WPM, 60–40 60% words	Voice resto-ration

Challenges and Ethical Concerns

Despite progress, hurdles persist:

- Accuracy and Bandwidth: Current systems excel at simple intents (e.g., cursor movement) but struggle with complex, unstructured thoughts due to noisy signals and limited neuron sampling.

- Invasiveness and Safety: Implants risk wire migration or tissue damage; non-invasive options like EEG lack precision. FDA approvals accelerated via "breakthrough" status, but long-term data is nascent.

- Ethics and Privacy: Potential for mind control or surveillance raises alarms—Neuralink faces SEC probes over animal testing. Experts emphasize consent-gated systems and bias audits to prevent misuse.

- Accessibility: High costs and surgical needs limit to trials; commercialization could take 2–5 years.

Future Outlook

By 2030, experts predict "telepathic" features like brain-to-brain messaging (e.g., via Neuralink networks) and AI "copilots" for thought enhancement. Integration with AR/VR and quantum computing could enable memory prosthetics or emotion sharing. As one analyst noted, today's BCIs are like the telegraph—functional but primitive; the "iPhone" era of seamless mind-machine symbiosis is imminent. This could redefine communication, but responsible development is crucial to avoid dystopian risks.

Time Travel Possibilities

Time travel, as popularly imagined—moving freely backward or forward in time like in science fiction—remains speculative and faces significant theoretical and practical hurdles. However, physics offers frameworks where specific forms of time travel might be possible, primarily within the constraints of general relativity and quantum mechanics. Below, I outline the leading theoretical possibilities, their challenges, and the current state of understanding.

Theoretical Pathways to Time Travel

1. Wormholes (Einstein-Rosen Bridges):

- Concept: General relativity permits wormholes— hypothetical tunnels connecting distant points in spacetime. If one end is accelerated or placed in a strong gravitational field, time dilation could make it a "time machine," allowing travel to the past or future relative to the other end.

- Mechanism: A traversable wormhole requires "exotic matter" with negative energy density to keep it open, as proposed by Kip Thorne's 1988 work. Quantum effects like the Casimir effect might provide such energy.

- Challenges:

  - No evidence of natural wormholes exists; creating one would require unimaginable energy.

  - Exotic matter is theoretical, with only small-scale quantum analogs observed.

- Stability issues: Wormholes might collapse instantly or create feedback loops (e.g., radiation buildup) that destroy them, per Hawking's chronology protection conjecture.

- Paradoxes: Traveling to the past risks "grandfather paradoxes," though solutions like the Novikov self-consistency principle suggest timelines adjust to prevent contradictions.

2. Closed Timelike Curves (CTCs):

- Concept: General relativity allows paths in spacetime where an object returns to its starting point, effectively traveling to the past. These arise in solutions like Gödel's rotating universe or near massive, spinning objects (e.g., Kerr black holes).

- Mechanism: A CTC could let you loop back to an earlier time, but only within specific spacetime geometries, like near a rapidly rotating black hole or a cosmic string.

- Challenges:

  - Requires extreme conditions (e.g., near a black hole's event horizon), inaccessible with current technology.

  - Hawking's conjecture suggests quantum effects might forbid CTCs to prevent paradoxes.

  - No experimental evidence; purely theoretical.

APPENDIX

3. Time Dilation (Forward Time Travel):

- Concept: General and special relativity show time passes slower in strong gravitational fields or at high speeds. This allows "forward" time travel by aging slower relative to others.

- Mechanism: Travel near a black hole or at near-light speeds, and decades could pass elsewhere while you experience minutes. Astronauts on the ISS already experience microseconds of this effect.

- Challenges:

  - Only allows forward travel, not backward.

  - Requires extreme speeds (approaching c) or proximity to massive objects, both technologically infeasible for significant jumps.

  - Energy costs for near-light-speed travel are astronomical (e.g., 10^{20} joules for a small craft).

4. Quantum Mechanics and Retrocausality:

- Concept: Some interpretations of quantum mechanics, like the transactional interpretation, suggest particles can influence the past via retrocausal effects. This could theoretically allow information transfer backward in time.

- Mechanism: Quantum entanglement or wavefunction collapse might enable "signals" to affect past states, potentially scaling to macroscopic effects.

- Challenges:

  - Highly speculative; no macroscopic retrocausality observed.

  - Limited to information, not physical travel.

  - Experimental tests (e.g., delayed-choice experiments) are inconclusive or small-scale.

Current State (2025)

- Theoretical Progress: Research in quantum gravity and string theory continues to explore CTCs and wormholes, but no breakthroughs confirm their feasibility. Papers in 2024–2025 (e.g., arXiv) propose quantum simulations of wormholes using entangled particles, but these are non-traversable and informational only.

- Experimental Limits: No direct evidence for time travel exists. Particle accelerators like CERN's LHC probe high-energy regimes, but nothing suggests time manipulation. Quantum computing advances (e.g., Google's 2025 qubit scaling) enable simulations of spacetime effects, but these are mathematical models, not physical time travel.

- Technological Barriers: Creating or accessing wormholes/CTCs requires energies on the order of 10^{44} joules (a star's output) or negative energy densities, far beyond current capabilities. Time dilation is real but impractical for significant leaps (e.g., a 1-year trip at 99.99% c yields only ~7 years forward).

APPENDIX

Practical and Philosophical Hurdles

- Energy and Engineering: Even if theoretically possible, the energy and precision needed for wormholes or CTCs are millennia beyond current technology. For context, stabilizing a 1-meter wormhole might require the mass-energy of Jupiter.

- Paradoxes: Backward time travel risks logical inconsistencies. Proposed resolutions (e.g., parallel universes, self-consistency) are untestable.

- Ethics and Control: If feasible, time travel could disrupt causality, history, or reality itself, raising existential risks. Regulatory frameworks would be critical.

Future Outlook

While forward time travel via time dilation is already real on tiny scales, backward time travel remains speculative, hinging on undiscovered physics (e.g., quantum gravity). Experts estimate practical time travel, if possible, is centuries away unless exotic matter or CTCs are found naturally. Speculative ideas like Alcubierre's warp drive or quantum tunneling through spacetime barriers are being studied but lack empirical grounding. For now, time travel is confined to theory and small-scale relativistic effects.

Theoretical Frameworks for Consciousness and Higher Dimensions

1. Higher-Dimensional Physics and Consciousness:

- **Concept: String theory and M-theory propose 10 or 11 spacetime dimensions, with extra dimensions "compactified" at subatomic scales. Some speculate consciousness might interact with these dimensions, as it remains unexplained by classical physics. For example, the Orch-OR theory (Penrose and Hameroff) suggests quantum processes in brain microtubules could link consciousness to fundamental spacetime structures, potentially accessing higher-dimensional information.**

- **Mechanism: Quantum coherence in neural structures might entangle with higher-dimensional quantum fields, allowing consciousness to "perceive" or process information beyond 4D spacetime. This could manifest as intuition, non-local awareness, or altered states.**

- Challenges:

  - No experimental evidence links microtubules to higher dimensions; Orch-OR remains controversial.

  - Extra dimensions are theoretical, detectable only at Planck-scale energies (10^{-35} meters), far beyond current technology like CERN's LHC.

  - Consciousness itself lacks a unified definition, complicating claims about dimensional interactions.

2. Non-Local Consciousness and Quantum Entanglement:

- **Concept: Some interpretations of quantum mechanics suggest consciousness might be non-local, meaning it could transcend spacetime constraints. Entanglement or quantum tunneling could theoretically allow consciousness to access information from higher-dimensional realms.**

- **Mechanism: If consciousness involves quantum effects (e.g., entangled particles in the brain), it might resonate with higher-dimensional quantum fields, as speculated in papers on quantum cognition (e.g., 2024 arXiv studies). This could enable phenomena like telepathy or precognition, interpreted as higher-dimensional connections.**

- Challenges:

  - Quantum effects in the brain are debated; warm, noisy environments typically disrupt coherence.

  - No evidence supports macroscopic quantum effects in consciousness.

  - Non-locality is informational, not physical, limiting practical "connection."

3. Altered States and Subjective Experience:

- Concept: Mystical experiences, meditation, or psychedelics (e.g., DMT) are often described as accessing "higher dimensions" or alternate realities. Neuroscientific studies suggest these states alter brain connectivity, potentially mimicking higher-dimensional perception.

- Mechanism: Hyperconnectivity in the brain's default mode network (DMN), observed in 2025 fMRI studies of psilocybin users, could create subjective experiences of expanded spacetime or universal unity. This might be interpreted as accessing higher dimensions, though it's likely neural rather than physical.

- Challenges:

  - Subjective experiences aren't evidence of physical higher dimensions.

  - Neural correlates (e.g., increased DMN activity) don't imply dimensional access, only altered perception.

  - Cultural and psychological factors shape these experiences, reducing objectivity.

4. Brain-Computer Interfaces and Simulated Dimensions:

- Concept: Advanced BCIs, like Neuralink's Telepathy or AlterEgo's 2025 headset, could simulate higher-dimensional interactions by decoding neural signals and interfacing with computational models of extra dimensions.

- Mechanism: BCIs could map brain activity to virtual environments with higher-dimensional geometries (e.g., 5D simulations in VR). AI-driven decoding (80% accuracy in 2025 EEG studies) might translate thoughts into interactions with these models, creating a "felt" connection to higher dimensions.

- Challenges:

  - Simulations are not physical access to higher dimensions, only representations.

  - BCI resolution limits complex thought decoding; current systems focus on motor or speech intents.

  - Computational power for real-time higher-dimensional modeling is insufficient.

Current State (2025)

- Scientific Progress: No direct evidence supports consciousness interacting with higher dimensions. Quantum consciousness models (e.g., Orch-OR) are unproven, with 2024–2025 experiments (e.g., quantum coherence in proteins) showing only microscale effects. String theory's extra dimensions remain untestable, with no breakthroughs from LHC or quantum computing.

- BCI Relevance: Neuralink's implants (7+ patients by 2025) and non-invasive BCIs (e.g., Meta's EEG caps) decode simple thoughts (100+ words per minute), but nothing suggests higher-dimensional access. They enhance communication, not metaphysical connections.

- Philosophical Context: Panpsychism and idealism propose consciousness as fundamental, potentially linked to all spacetime dimensions, but these are untestable hypotheses. Recent X posts (September 2025) discuss DMT-induced "hyperdimensional" visions, but these are anecdotal, not scientific.

APPENDIX

Challenges and Limitations

- Empirical Gaps: Higher dimensions are theoretical; no detectors (e.g., LIGO, LHC) have found them. Consciousness studies lack consensus on neural correlates, let alone dimensional links.

- Energy Scales: Accessing extra dimensions requires Planck-scale energies (10^{19} GeV), far beyond current capabilities (LHC reaches ~14 TeV).

- Subjectivity: Experiences of "higher dimensions" are often psychological or cultural, not physical.

- Paradoxes: If consciousness could access higher dimensions, it might disrupt causality or create untestable effects, complicating scientific validation.

Future Outlook:
By 2030–2040, advances in quantum computing, BCIs, and neuroscience might clarify quantum consciousness or simulate higher-dimensional interactions. For example, quantum simulations of wormholes (2025 Google experiments) could model dimensional effects, potentially interfacing with BCIs. However, physical access to higher dimensions likely requires breakthroughs in unified physics, possibly centuries away. [*This apparently ignores effects of technology acceleration due to cross-technology interactions.*] Meditation, psychedelics, or BCIs might enhance subjective experiences of "higher realms," but these remain neural, not dimensional.

Frequency Of Occurrence Of ESP Phenomena

Reports of ESP (extrasensory perception) phenomena, such as telepathy, clairvoyance, or precognition, are relatively common in anecdotal accounts but lack consistent empirical validation. Surveys and studies provide some insight into their prevalence:

- Public Belief and Self-Reported Experiences: Polls consistently show a significant portion of the population believes in or claims to have experienced ESP. For example, a 2005 Gallup poll found 41% of Americans believed in ESP, with 26% reporting they had experienced telepathy or clairvoyance-like events. Similar surveys, like a 2014 YouGov poll, indicate about 20-30% of people claim to have had a "psychic" experience, such as premonitions or unexplained intuitions.

- Parapsychological Research: Studies in parapsychology, such as those conducted by the Rhine Research Center or the University of Edinburgh's Koestler Parapsychology Unit, document thousands of anecdotal reports of ESP phenomena. However, controlled experiments (e.g., Ganzfeld studies) yield mixed results, with effect sizes often small (around 0.1-0.2 standard deviations above chance) and heavily debated due to methodological issues.

- Cultural and Historical Context: Reports of ESP-like phenomena are widespread across cultures and history, from ancient oracles to modern psychic claims. For instance, indigenous cultures often describe shamanic visions, while contemporary accounts include "psychic" predictions or intuitive experiences. These are often tied to cultural frameworks, making raw numbers hard to quantify globally.

- Skeptical Perspective: Critics argue many reports stem from cognitive biases (e.g., confirmation bias, the Barnum effect) or statistical coincidences. The lack of reproducible evidence under controlled conditions means mainstream science often dismisses ESP claims, though public interest persists.

Exact numbers are tough to pin down due to varying definitions of ESP and reliance on self-reporting. Roughly 1 in 4 people in Western countries claim some form of ESP experience, but scientific consensus leans heavily toward skepticism.

Edgar Cayce Profile

Edgar Cayce (March 18, 1877 - January 3, 1945) was an American clairvoyant, self-proclaimed faith healer, and psychic often called the "Sleeping Prophet." Born near Hopkinsville, Kentucky, to a modest family—his father was a failed farmer turned dry-goods store operator—he discovered his abilities as a young man after losing his voice and using hypnosis to diagnose and heal himself. Cayce sought a simple Christian life but became renowned for entering trance states to provide insights, despite initial reluctance about his gifts.

Key Activities and Contributions

Cayce's work spanned over 40 years, during which he gave approximately 14,000 documented "readings" while in an unconscious, sleep-like state. These sessions involved lying down, closing his eyes, and answering questions posed by others, with responses transcribed verbatim. He collaborated with professionals like osteopath Al Layne and homeopath Wesley Ketchum early on.

- Medical Diagnoses and Holistic Healing: The majority of readings (about 9,000) focused on diagnosing illnesses and prescribing remedies, often using unconventional holistic approaches like diet, herbs, and spinal adjustments. He is credited with influencing modern holistic medicine, with case studies showing successes in treating epilepsy, arthritis, scleroderma, and eye injuries. Cayce emphasized the mind-body connection and reincarnation as factors in health.

- Psychic and Metaphysical Insights: Beyond medicine, readings covered reincarnation, past lives, Atlantis, ancient Egypt, dream interpretation, and prophecies (e.g., predicting world events like stock market crashes and wars). He explored philosophy, metaphysics, and esoteric topics, such as the differences between spirit and soul, at the request of associates like printer Arthur Lammers.

- Business Ventures and Challenges: In the 1920s, Cayce dabbled in oil drilling to fund a hospital, which failed. He moved frequently, settling in Virginia Beach, Virginia, in the 1930s after his readings advised it.

Legacy and Organizations Founded

In 1931, Cayce established the Association for Research and Enlightenment (A.R.E.) in Virginia Beach as a non-profit to preserve and study his readings. It includes a library, vault for transcripts, and promotes research in psychic phenomena, health, and spirituality without opposing any religion. By the late 20th century, A.R.E. had around 30,000 members worldwide, fueling New Age thought. His sons, Hugh Lynn and Edgar Evans, expanded the organization during and after World War II.

Biographies like Thomas Sugrue's There Is a River (1942)—the only one published in his lifetime—brought fame, detailing his life and "miracle cures." Posthumously, works like Jess Stearn's The Sleeping Prophet (1967) and Sidney Kirkpatrick's Edgar Cayce: An American Prophet (2000) analyzed his archives. Cayce's influence persists in alternative medicine, spirituality, and media, though skeptics attribute his knowledge to absorbed information rather than supernatural sources.

Cayce died in 1945 from a stroke, exacerbated by overwork (up to eight readings daily). His work remains controversial but inspirational, blending Christianity with mysticism.

APPENDIX

The Free Will Vs. Divine Foreknowledge Paradox

This a theological and philosophical puzzle that arises when trying to reconcile human free will with the concept of an omniscient deity who knows all future events:

The Paradox

- Free Will: Humans have the ability to make choices freely, without being determined by prior causes or external forces. This implies that individuals are responsible for their actions and could have chosen otherwise.

- Divine Foreknowledge: An omniscient God knows everything, including all future events and human choices, before they happen. This knowledge is often considered infallible and complete.

- The Conflict: If God knows with certainty what a person will do in the future, it seems their choice is predetermined, undermining free will. If a person could choose differently, it seems to challenge God's omniscience, as God's knowledge would be incorrect.

Key Points of the Paradox

- If God's foreknowledge is certain, a person's actions appear fixed, suggesting they lack the freedom to act otherwise.

- If humans have free will and can choose differently, God's foreknowledge might be fallible, which contradicts the idea of divine omniscience.

- The paradox questions whether free will and divine foreknowledge can logically coexist.

Proposed Resolutions

Philosophers and theologians have offered several approaches to address this paradox:

1. Boethian Solution (Timelessness):

- Proposed by Boethius, this view holds that God exists outside of time and perceives all moments (past, present, future) simultaneously in an eternal "now."

- God's knowledge doesn't "foreknow" events in a temporal sense but sees them as present. Thus, God's knowledge of a choice doesn't causally determine it, preserving free will.

- Critique: This assumes a non-temporal view of God, which some find abstract or incompatible with a personal deity interacting with the world.

2. Molinism (Middle Knowledge):

- Developed by Luis de Molina, this view posits that God has "middle knowledge" of all possible outcomes, including what free creatures would choose in any given circumstance (called counterfactuals of freedom).

- God knows what you would freely choose in any situation and creates a world where those choices align with His plan, maintaining both divine knowledge and human freedom.

- Critique: Critics argue that knowing what a person would freely do still implies a form of determinism, and the concept of middle knowledge is debated for its logical coherence.

3. Open Theism:

- Open theists argue that God's omniscience doesn't include exhaustive knowledge of future free choices. Instead, God knows all possibilities and the present perfectly but leaves the future "open" for free agents to determine.

- This preserves free will by limiting divine foreknowledge to what is logically knowable, treating future free choices as indeterminate.

- Critique: This view is controversial because it challenges traditional notions of divine omniscience, suggesting God doesn't know the future exhaustively.

4. Compatibilism:

- Compatibilists argue that free will and divine foreknowledge are compatible because free will doesn't require the ability to do otherwise in an absolute sense, but only the ability to act according to one's desires and reasons.

- God's foreknowledge doesn't cause the choice; it simply knows it. A person can still act freely in the sense that their choices align with their will, even if God knows them in advance.

- Critique: Critics argue this redefines free will in a way that feels like soft determinism, as the outcome is still fixed from God's perspective.

5. Logical Distinction (Non-Causal Knowledge):

- Some argue that divine foreknowledge is not causal. God's knowing a future event doesn't force it to happen; it's like knowing the sun will rise tomorrow without causing it.

- Free will remains intact because God's knowledge depends on what the person freely chooses, not vice versa.

- Critique: This doesn't fully resolve the sense that certain knowledge implies a fixed outcome, which feels restrictive to some interpretations of freedom.

Ongoing Debate

- The paradox hinges on definitions of free will, omniscience, and time. Libertarian free will (total freedom to choose otherwise) creates more tension with divine foreknowledge than compatibilist views.

- Different religious traditions (e.g., Christianity, Islam) approach the paradox variably, with some emphasizing divine sovereignty (e.g., predestination in Calvinism) and others prioritizing human responsibility.

- Philosophers like Augustine, Aquinas, and modern thinkers continue to debate whether the paradox is resolvable or if it reflects a mystery beyond human understanding.

APPENDIX

Conclusion

The Free Will vs. Divine Foreknowledge paradox challenges us to grapple with the nature of freedom, divine attributes, and the structure of reality. Solutions like Boethianism, Molinism, open theism, and compatibilism offer ways to reconcile the two, but each has trade-offs and depends on specific assumptions about God, time, and human agency. The debate remains open, with no universally accepted resolution.

APPENDIX

Prophecy In Deuteronomy 28

*DEUTERONOMY. 28:15 But it shall come to pass, if thou wilt not hearken unto the voice of the LORD thy God, to observe to do all His commandments and His statutes which I command thee this day; that all these curses shall come upon thee, and overtake thee. ... :20 The LORD will send upon thee cursing, discomfiture, and rebuke, in all that thou puttest thy hand unto to do, until thou be destroyed, and until thou perish quickly; because of the evil of thy doings, whereby thou hast forsaken Me. ...:48 **therefore shalt thou serve thine enemy whom the LORD shall send against thee, in hunger, and in thirst, and in nakedness, and in want of all things; and he shall put a yoke of iron upon thy neck, until he have destroyed thee. :49 The LORD will bring a nation against thee from far, from the end of the earth, as the vulture swoopeth down; a nation whose tongue thou shalt not understand;** :50 a nation of fierce countenance, that shall not regard the person of the old, nor show favour to the young. **:51 And he shall eat the fruit of thy cattle, and the fruit of thy ground, until thou be destroyed; that also shall not leave thee corn** [i.e., grain, not maize], **wine, or oil, the increase of thy kine, or the young of thy flock, until he have caused thee to perish. :52 And he shall besiege thee in all thy gates, until thy high and fortified walls come down, wherein thou didst trust, throughout all thy land; and he shall besiege thee in all thy gates throughout all thy land, which the LORD thy God hath given thee.** :53 And thou shalt eat the fruit of thine own body, the flesh of thy sons and of thy daughters whom the LORD thy God hath given thee; in the siege and in the straitness, wherewith thine enemies shall straiten thee ... :62 And ye shall be left few in number, whereas ye were as the stars of heaven for multitude; because thou didst not hearken unto the voice of the LORD thy God. :63 And it shall come to pass, that as the LORD rejoiced over you to do you good, and to multiply you; so the LORD will rejoice over* *you to cause you to perish, and to destroy you;* **and ye shall be plucked from off the land whither thou goest in to possess it. :64 And the LORD shall scatter thee among all peoples, from the one end of the earth even unto the other end of the earth; and there thou shalt serve other gods, which thou hast not known, thou nor thy fathers, even wood and stone.** *:65 And among these nations shalt thou have no repose, and there shall be no rest for the sole of thy foot; but the LORD shall give thee there a trembling heart, and failing of eyes, and languishing of soul. :66 And thy life shall hang in doubt before thee; and thou shalt fear night and day, and shalt have no assurance of thy life. :67 In the morning thou shalt say: 'Would it were even!' and at even thou shalt say: 'Would it were morning!' for the fear of thy heart which thou shalt fear, and for the sight of thine eyes which thou shalt see.* **:68 And the LORD shall bring thee back into Egypt in ships, by the way whereof I said unto thee: 'Thou shalt see it no more again';** *and there ye shall sell yourselves unto your enemies for bondmen and for bondwoman, and no man shall buy you.*

Scriptural Assertions As To Why God Created The Universe

The Talmud, a central text in Rabbinic Judaism, does not provide a single, definitive assertion about why God created the universe, as it focuses more on legal, ethical, and narrative discussions than on systematic theology. However, various Talmudic passages, along with related Jewish philosophical and mystical traditions (e.g., Midrash and Kabbalah), offer insights into possible reasons for creation. Below are key Talmudic and related Jewish perspectives on why God created the universe, presented concisely:

1. To Manifest Divine Goodness: The Talmud (e.g., Megillah 14a) and later Jewish philosophers like Maimonides suggest that God created the universe as an expression of His inherent goodness. A benevolent God creates to share His goodness with beings capable of receiving it, particularly humans who can emulate divine attributes like kindness and justice.

2. For Humanity to Partner in Creation: The Talmud (Shabbat 10a, 119b) implies that God created the world to enable humans to engage in acts of righteousness (tzedakah) and Torah study, perfecting the world through moral and spiritual partnership with God. The concept of tikkun olam (repairing the world) emerges from this idea.

3. To Establish a Dwelling Place in the Lower Worlds: In Midrash Tanchuma (Nasso 7:1), a text closely related to Talmudic thought, it is suggested that God desired a "dwelling place" in the physical world. The universe was created so that humanity, through free will and adherence to mitzvot (commandments), could transform the material world into a space where divine presence is manifest.

4. For Divine Glory and Recognition: The Talmud (Berachot 6a) and Midrash (Genesis Rabbah 1:5) indicate that creation serves to reveal God's glory. By creating a universe with beings capable of recognizing and praising Him, God's attributes (e.g., mercy, justice) are made known.

5. For the Sake of Israel and Torah: Some Talmudic and Midrashic sources (e.g., Genesis Rabbah 1:4, Sifrei Deuteronomy 36) assert that the universe was created for the sake of Israel and the Torah, which serve as the spiritual blueprint and purpose of existence. This reflects the idea that the moral and covenantal relationship between God and Israel is central to creation's purpose.

6. *To Enable Free Will and Moral Choice: The Talmud (e.g., Eruvin 100b) emphasizes human free will as a core component of existence. God created the universe to provide a stage for humans to exercise free will, choosing between good and evil, thereby earning spiritual reward and fulfilling divine purpose.*

Notes:

- The Talmud rarely addresses metaphysical questions directly, so these ideas are often inferred from aggadic (narrative) sections or elaborated in later Jewish thought (e.g., by Rashi, Nachmanides, or Kabbalistic works like the Zohar).

- Jewish tradition generally avoids dogmatic assertions about God's motives, emphasizing instead human responsibility within creation.

APPENDIX

Scriptural View Of The Interaction Of Heaven And Earth

Jewish scriptures, primarily the Torah, Talmud, and later mystical texts like the Kabbalah, offer a complex view of the relationship between Heaven and Earth, emphasizing a dynamic interplay where actions in one realm influence the other. The following points summarize key perspectives:

1. Torah and Tanakh (Hebrew Bible):

- Divine Influence on Earth: The Torah portrays God as actively involved in earthly events, responding to human actions. For example, in Deuteronomy 11:13-17, obedience to God's commandments brings blessings like rain and prosperity, while disobedience leads to drought and punishment, suggesting a direct link between human behavior and divine action in Heaven affecting Earth.

- Human Actions Impacting Heaven: Human righteousness or sin is believed to affect the spiritual realm. For instance, in Genesis 6:5-7, human wickedness grieves God's heart, prompting the flood, indicating that earthly actions resonate in the divine realm. Similarly, collective repentance, as in Jonah 3:10 with Nineveh, can alter divine decrees.

- Covenantal Relationship: The covenant (e.g., with Abraham in Genesis 17) establishes a reciprocal relationship. Human adherence to the covenant influences divine favor, while divine promises shape earthly outcomes, like the giving of the Land of Israel.

APPENDIX

2. Talmud and Rabbinic Literature:

- The Talmud expands on this interplay, teaching that human actions, particularly mitzvot (commandments) and prayer, can influence heavenly decrees. For example, in Berakhot 32a, prayer is said to have the power to annul harsh divine judgments.

- The concept of "measure for measure" (*middah k'neged middah*) suggests that earthly actions provoke corresponding responses from Heaven. A person's charity, for instance, might elicit divine mercy (Shabbat 151b).

- The Talmud also describes angels reporting earthly events to God (e.g., Chagigah 5b), reinforcing the idea that human conduct is observed and impacts divine decisions.

3. Kabbalistic and Mystical Perspectives:

- In Kabbalah, particularly the Zohar, Heaven and Earth are deeply interconnected through the sefirot (divine attributes). Human actions, especially mitzvot, strengthen the flow of divine energy (*shefa*) from Heaven to Earth, sustaining the world. Conversely, sins disrupt this flow, causing spiritual and earthly imbalance (Zohar I:77b).

- The concept of "as above, so below" suggests that earthly events mirror heavenly realities. For example, unity among the Jewish people on Earth fosters unity in the heavenly realms, enhancing divine blessings (Tikkunei Zohar 21).

- Mystics also believe that human intention (*kavanah*) during prayer or rituals can elevate earthly actions to influence higher spiritual worlds, repairing cosmic flaws (*tikkun olam*).

4. Prophetic and Eschatological Views:

- Prophets like Isaiah and Jeremiah link earthly behavior to divine intervention. For instance, Isaiah 1:11-17 critiques empty rituals, urging justice to align Earth with Heaven's will, implying that moral conduct shapes divine response.

- In messianic visions (e.g., Isaiah 11:6-9), earthly harmony reflects a perfected heavenly order, suggesting that events on Earth can herald or delay messianic redemption, impacting the divine plan.

In summary, Jewish scriptures depict a reciprocal relationship where human actions—mitzvot, prayer, or sin—directly influence divine responses in Heaven, which in turn affect earthly outcomes like blessings, punishments, or cosmic harmony. Mystical traditions deepen this by portraying human deeds as shaping spiritual realms, with Earth and Heaven in constant dialogue.

Scriptural Sources For "The Universe Was Created For The Sake Of Humanity"

The idea that the universe was created for the sake of humanity is a significant concept in Jewish thought, particularly in rabbinic and mystical traditions. While no single verse in the Torah explicitly states, "the universe was created for the sake of man," several scriptural sources, along with their interpretations in the Talmud, Midrash, and Kabbalah, support this idea. Below are key Jewish scriptural sources and their interpretations that articulate or imply this concept:

1. Torah (Genesis):

- Genesis 1:26-28: "And God said, 'Let us make man in our image, after our likeness, and let them have dominion over the fish of the sea, and over the birds of the air, and over the cattle, and over all the earth...' And God blessed them, and God said to them, 'Be fruitful and multiply, and fill the earth and subdue it...'"

  - Interpretation: This passage establishes humanity as the pinnacle of creation, granted dominion over the earth. Rabbinic commentators, such as Rashi, infer that humanity's unique creation in God's image and its role as stewards of creation suggest that the world was designed with humanity's purpose in mind.

- Genesis 2:15: "The Lord God took the man and put him in the Garden of Eden to work it and keep it."

  - Interpretation: The placement of Adam in the Garden to tend it implies that the world was created as an environment for human responsibility and purpose, reinforcing humanity's centrality.

2. Talmud:

- Sanhedrin 37a: "Whoever saves a single life is considered as if they saved an entire world."

  - Interpretation: This teaching, derived from the story of Cain and Abel (Genesis 4:10), implies that each human life is of cosmic significance, suggesting that the universe's purpose is tied to human existence and moral actions.

- Shabbat 77b: Rabbi Yehuda says, "Everything that was created in the six days of creation needs improvement... and the first man was created last to show that if he is worthy, all of creation is for his sake."

  - Interpretation: This explicitly states that the universe's creation culminates in humanity, and if a person is righteous, all of creation exists to serve their spiritual purpose.

3. Midrash:

- Midrash Rabbah (Genesis 8:1): "Rabbi Yehoshua ben Levi said: All the acts of creation were created for the honor of man."

  - Interpretation: This midrashic teaching directly links the purpose of creation to humanity's honor, suggesting that the universe's vastness exists to elevate human potential and responsibility.

- Midrash Tanchuma (Tazria 5): "The Holy One, blessed be He, created the world for the sake of Israel, and Israel for the sake of the Torah."

  - Interpretation: This extends the idea to suggest that humanity, particularly the Jewish people, and their engagement with the Torah are the ultimate purpose of creation, tying the universe's existence to human spiritual fulfillment.

4. Kabbalistic Sources:

- Zohar (Zohar I:134a): "The Holy One, blessed be He, looked into the Torah and created the world, and the world was created for the sake of Israel, who would accept the Torah."

  - Interpretation: In Kabbalah, the universe's creation is purposeful, designed to enable humanity (specifically Israel) to fulfill the divine will through Torah and mitzvot, positioning humanity as the focal point of creation.

- Tikkunei Zohar (Introduction): The universe is sustained by human actions, particularly through righteous deeds and prayer, which channel divine energy (shefa) into the world.

  - Interpretation: This implies that the universe's ongoing existence and harmony depend on human spiritual activity, reinforcing the idea that creation exists for humanity's sake.

  -

5. Philosophical and Rabbinic Commentary:

- Maimonides (Rambam, Guide for the Perplexed, 3:13): Maimonides argues that while the universe has its own intrinsic purpose in reflecting God's glory, humanity's intellectual and moral capacity gives it a central role in fulfilling divine intentions.

  - Interpretation: Humanity's ability to know and serve God positions it as a key purpose of creation, though Maimonides cautions against an overly anthropocentric view.

- Nachmanides (Ramban, Commentary on Genesis 1:26): Nachmanides emphasizes that humanity's creation in God's image grants it a unique role, with the world designed to support human spiritual growth.

Summary:
The notion that "the universe was created for the sake of man" is supported by the Torah's depiction of humanity's dominion and purpose (Genesis 1:26-28, 2:15), reinforced by Talmudic teachings (Sanhedrin 37a, Shabbat 77b), Midrashic interpretations (Genesis Rabbah 8:1, Tanchuma Tazria 5), and Kabbalistic views (Zohar I:134a). These sources collectively suggest that humanity, through its moral, spiritual, and intellectual capacities—especially in fulfilling the Torah—gives purpose to the universe, with creation designed to enable human righteousness and connection to God.

Logical Principle Supporting Sinai Revelation Credibility

We can generalize the operative concept to say, *one cannot successfully **falsely** assert that an **extremely dramatic, traumatically attention-demanding event** occurred before the **entire population** of a society.* ("Successfully" here means that the teller convinces the *vast majority* of listeners that the assertion is true, and *it becomes part of the culture of the listeners.*) This is because such a false assertion would conflict with the existing lack of corroborating evidence for the assertion.

Now, recasting the principle in If-Then form, it says*: If an assertion about an **extremely dramatic traumatically attention-demanding event** occurring before the **entire population** of a society is false, then the assertion will not (generally, widely) be believed.* Why this recasting? Well, if you recall in high school geometry or logic class, you can have an If-Then proposition, say "If A, then B". There are then three other derivatives of this proposition, viz:

Proposition:	If A, then B
Converse:	If B, then A
Inverse:	If not-A, then not-B
Contrapositive:	If not-B, then not-A.

Example:

Proposition: If it is raining, then the sky is cloudy.
(Let's assume this proposition is true.)

Converse:　　　　　If the sky is cloudy, then it is raining. (This might be false, the sky might be cloudy without rain.)

Inverse:　　　　　If it is not raining, then the sky is not cloudy. (Also possibly false, just as with the Converse)

Contrapositive:　　　If the sky is not cloudy, then it is not raining. (This would have to be true.)

Logical analysis tells us that if the Proposition is true, then the truth of the Converse and Inverse are not determined given the original proposition alone, but the Contrapositive *will* be true. In fact, *a Proposition and its Contrapositive are logically equivalent*, i.e., they will be either both true or both false (together).

Back to our case:

A = "assertion [*about an **extremely dramatic traumatically attention-demanding event** occurring before the **entire population** of a society*] is false"

B = "assertion [*about an **extremely dramatic traumatically attention-demanding event** occurring before the **entire population** of a society*] will not be believed".

OK, the contrapositive of our principle will now be: *If an assertion about an **extremely dramatic traumatically attention-demanding event** occurring before the **entire population** of a society **is** (generally, widely) believed (in that society), **then the assertion is true**.* This is a rather astounding result! It says, for example, that if there is a widespread belief in our society that an earthquake destroyed San Francisco in 1906, then that widespread belief is, ***in itself***, *prima facie* evidence that the event actually took place. The reason is, if the event didn't take place, no such widespread belief could have arisen. *The crux of this argument centers around the requirement that the event being asserted* is an **extremely dramatic, traumatically attention-demanding occurrence happening before the *entire* population of a society**, such as a major earthquake.

There are few such events about which this discussion would be relevant. They would normally be natural disasters. In other words, if *EVERYONE* in a society believes that a miraculous or highly unusual **extremely dramatic, traumatically attention-demanding** event *PUBLICLY* took place before the *ENTIRE* population of that society, then that's *prima facie* evidence that the event actually took place. This is a variant of Abraham Lincoln's *"You can't fool all the people all the time"* aphorism.

A further implication of this principle is that *if this specific type of assertion is widely believed about an event in the past and no other evidence of this event exists in the present, then the existence of the belief is, in itself, an indication that the corroborating evidence at one time **did** exist.* Again, this is necessary because without that corroborating evidence, the belief could not have arisen and become widely accepted. This is a very powerful principle for historical analysis. It allows us to infer that a certain historical event actually did occur despite lack of historical documentation that might otherwise normally be required in such cases, as long as it fulfills the proper requirements:

- The event is a miraculous or highly unusual **extremely dramatic, traumatically attention-demanding** occurrence.

- The event took place *PUBLICLY*.

- The event took place before the ***ENTIRE*** population of the society in question.

- It is possible at least to identify a point in the past, if not at present, where the entire population of the society believed that the event took place.

Again, these criteria are *very* restrictive. For example, this does ***NOT*** apply to "Everyone knows" statements in general, such as *"Everyone knows the Earth is flat and you'll fall off the edge,"* which, at one time, most everyone in Western society might have believed. There was no alleged ***UNIVERSAL PUBLIC*** witness of any **extremely dramatic, traumatically attention-demanding event** involved in this type of assertion. In fact, this argument doesn't apply to most propositions that are widely believed. This is because very few things about which we hold beliefs involve any **extremely dramatic, traumatically attention-demanding occurrence happening before the *entire* population of a society.**

Normally, natural disasters would be the only kinds of events to which this analysis would apply. There is, however, one historical event other than a natural disaster to which this analysis is also relevant. This was when God came down on Mt. Sinai and appeared before the entire nation of Israel to give the Ten Commandments. Here we have an assertion about an **extremely dramatic traumatically attention-demanding event** (See Exo. 19-20) **occurring before the entire population** of the society of the nation of Israel, which assertion, historically, until only early in the 19th century, was accepted as Truth by the entire society of the Jewish People.

Scriptural Sources For The Concept That God Continuously Creates Or Sustains The Universe

The concept that God continuously creates or sustains the universe, actively maintaining its existence, is a fundamental idea in Jewish theology, particularly emphasized in rabbinic, philosophical, and mystical texts. This notion, often referred to as *hashgacha* (divine providence) or continuous creation, suggests that the universe depends on God's ongoing will to exist at every moment. Below are key Jewish scriptural sources and their interpretations that support this concept:

1. Torah (Tanach):

   - Genesis 1:1: "In the beginning, God created the heavens and the earth."

     - Interpretation: While this verse describes the initial act of creation, later Jewish thinkers, such as Maimonides and Nachmanides, argue that the verb "created" (bara) implies an ongoing divine act. The universe's existence is not self-sustaining but relies on God's continuous creative will.

   - Psalms 104:29-30: "When You hide Your face, they [creatures] are terrified; when You take away their breath, they die and return to dust. When You send Your Spirit, they are created, and You renew the face of the earth."

     - Interpretation: This explicitly describes God's active role in sustaining life. The renewal of creation through God's "Spirit" (*ruach*) suggests that existence is continually dependent on divine power. The Midrash (Genesis Rabbah 10:7) expands on this, stating that God renews creation daily.

- Isaiah 40:28: "Do you not know? Have you not heard? The Lord is the everlasting God, the Creator of the ends of the earth. He does not faint or grow weary; His understanding is unsearchable."

  - Interpretation: This verse underscores God's unending creative power, implying that His role as Creator is not a one-time act but an ongoing process that sustains the universe.

2. Talmud and Rabbinic Literature:

- Chagigah 12b: "Rabbi Yochanan said: Every day, God renews the work of creation."

  - Interpretation: This Talmudic statement directly supports the idea of continuous creation, suggesting that God actively sustains the universe daily, without which it would cease to exist.

- Berakhot 58a: The blessing "Who renews the work of creation" (recited in the daily prayers) reflects the belief that God's creative act is ongoing, maintaining the natural order moment by moment.

  - Interpretation: This liturgical practice, rooted in rabbinic tradition, reinforces the concept that the universe's existence depends on God's constant renewal.

3. Midrash:

- Genesis Rabbah 10:7: "Every moment, God renews His creation, as it is written, 'Who renews the face of the earth' (Psalms 104:30)."

    - Interpretation: This midrash explicitly ties the renewal of creation to God's ongoing act, suggesting that the universe would revert to nothingness without divine sustenance.

- Midrash Tehillim (Psalms) 104:2: "God wraps Himself in light as with a garment... He renews the creation every day."

    - Interpretation: This emphasizes that God's creative power is not static but dynamic, continuously upholding the cosmos.

4. Kabbalistic and Mystical Texts:

- Zohar (Zohar I:5a): "The Holy One, blessed be He, sustains the world with His will, and if He were to withdraw His will for a single moment, all existence would return to nothingness."

    - Interpretation: The Zohar articulates a mystical view of continuous creation, where God's will (expressed through the sefirot, divine attributes) actively sustains the universe. The concept of shefa (divine flow) implies that God's energy constantly pours into creation to maintain its existence.

- Tikkunei Zohar 70: "Each moment, the world is created anew by the utterance of God."

- Interpretation: This reflects the idea that the divine speech (as in Genesis 1, "And God said") continues to sustain reality, echoing the ten utterances of creation in a perpetual process.

5. Philosophical Sources:

- Maimonides (Rambam, Guide for the Perplexed, 2:1): Maimonides argues that the universe's existence depends on God's continuous will. He writes, "The existence of all things depends on Him, and if He ceased to exist, all would cease to exist."

  - Interpretation: Maimonides frames continuous creation as a philosophical necessity, emphasizing that God's active causation is required at every moment for the universe to persist.

- Nachmanides (Ramban, Commentary on Genesis 1:1): Nachmanides explains that God's creation is not a one-time event but a constant act of bringing existence from nothingness (ex nihilo), as the universe has no independent existence apart from God.

  - Interpretation: This view aligns with the mystical idea that God's power continuously upholds the cosmos.

6. Liturgical Reinforcement:

- Morning Prayer (Yotzer Or): The daily prayer includes the phrase, "Who in His goodness renews the work of creation every day, continually."

- Interpretation: This prayer, rooted in Psalms 104 and Talmudic teachings, reflects the widespread Jewish belief in God's ongoing creative act as essential to the universe's existence.

Summary:
Jewish scriptures and their interpretations articulate the concept of continuous creation through key sources: Psalms 104:29-30 and Isaiah 40:28 in the Tanakh emphasize God's active role in sustaining existence; Talmudic passages (Chagigah 12b, Berakhot 58a) and Midrash (Genesis Rabbah 10:7) describe daily renewal; Kabbalistic texts (Zohar I:5a, Tikkunei Zohar 70) portray God's will as perpetually sustaining the cosmos; and philosophical works by Maimonides and Nachmanides argue for the universe's dependence on God's ongoing creative power. Together, these sources affirm that the universe's existence relies on God's continuous act of creation, without which it would cease to be.

Overview of Mind Uploading Research

Mind uploading, also known as whole brain emulation (WBE), refers to the hypothetical process of scanning a biological brain in sufficient detail to replicate its structure and function in a digital substrate, effectively transferring consciousness or cognitive processes to a computer. This concept bridges neuroscience, computer science, and philosophy, with potential applications in immortality, space travel, and cognitive enhancement. As of September 2025, mind uploading remains speculative and theoretical—no successful human mind transfers have occurred, and the technology is far from practical realization. However, foundational research in related fields like brain mapping, simulation, and brain-computer interfaces (BCIs) is advancing rapidly, driven by AI, computing power, and neurotech investments.

Current State: Theoretical Foundations and Incremental Progress

- Core Challenges: The human brain comprises ~86 billion neurons and ~100 trillion synapses, with dynamic states influenced by biochemistry, quantum effects, and environmental factors. Scanning at this resolution non-destructively is impossible with current tech; destructive methods (e.g., slicing and imaging) raise identity concerns (e.g., is the upload "you" or a copy?). Simulations require exascale computing, and consciousness transfer assumes functionalism (mind as software), which is debated—some argue it's tied to biology.

- Feasibility Estimates: Optimists like Ray Kurzweil predict non-invasive merging with AI (via nanoscale sensors) by the 2030s, with full uploads by 2045. Pessimists, including neuroscientists, estimate 100–200 years due to unresolved issues in consciousness and data fidelity. A 2025 study in Synthese critiques "uploading optimism," noting that simulations might create multiples, not true continuity.

Key Research Areas and Recent Developments

Research focuses on prerequisites: brain mapping (connectomics), emulation (simulation), and interfaces (BCIs). Here's a breakdown:

Area	Description	2025 Milestones	Key Players/ Projects
Connectomics (Brain Mapping)	Creating detailed neural wiring diagrams (connectomes). Essential for emulation blueprints.	- Human brain mapping efforts (e.g., EU's €600M project) failed to fully describe structure, let alone dynamic states. - Advances in fMRI and two-photon microscopy visualize connections with better detail, but at <1% resolution for full brains.	- Blue Brain Project (EPFL): Simulates mammalian brain sections. - NIH BRAIN Initiative: Targets whole-brain functional imaging by 2025, with 2mm resolution scans in <1 second for resting-state networks.

| Whole Brain Emulation (Simulation) | Running brain models on supercomputers to mimic cognition. | - Exponential supercomputer growth enables larger simulations (e.g., mouse-scale by 2024), but human-scale needs 10^18 FLOPS— projected feasible by 2030s via trends. - 2023 Foresight Workshop revisited WBE roadmap; AI acceleration shortens timelines, but no human trials. - Preprint on dendritic engrams (memory storage) advances functional data for emulation. | - Carboncopies Foundation: Leads WBE R&D; 2025 workshop on "functionalizing brain data" using AI-generated ground-truth. - OpenWorm: Full C. elegans (302-neuron worm) emulation, scaling toward mammals. |
| | | Workshop revisited WBE roadmap; AI acceleration shortens timelines, but no human trials. - Preprint on dendritic engrams (memory storage) advances functional data for emulation. | |

Brain-Computer Interfaces (BCIs)	Non-invasive/invasive tech for thought-to-action; a stepping stone to uploads via gradual neuron replacement ("Ship of Theseus").	- ~25 clinical trials underway; implants last up to 15 years. - Non-invasive: Meta's 2025 papers decode thoughts to text at 80% accuracy in real-time using fMRI/EEG—no whispering needed. - Invasive: Neuralink (5 paralyzed users control devices by thought, June 2025); Synchron's Stentrode (endovascular, FDA pivotal trial 2025). - UT Austin's AI decoder translates fMRI to text after 1-hour training; Carnegie Mellon's AI decodes intentions for virtual object control.	- Neuralink, Synchron, Neuracle: Expanding trials for speech/movement restoration. - Precision Neuroscience: FDA-cleared Layer 7 ECoG implant (30-day use, April 2025).

- Notable 2025 Breakthroughs:

  - Thought-to-Text/Speech: A BCI implant decodes silent thoughts into speech in 3 seconds (Nature Neuroscience), using wedding video audio to mimic the patient's voice—18 years post-stroke.

  - Privacy Features: UC Davis's mental "password" BCI activates decoding only on command, addressing surveillance fears.

  - Non-Invasive Scaling: Meta/UT Austin systems reduce training to 1 hour; 74% accuracy in predicting thoughts from a 125,000-word vocabulary (NPR, August 2025).

Major Projects and Investments

- Carboncopies Foundation: Focuses on WBE for preserving brain function; offers due diligence for neurotech investors. Hosts ethics panels on emulation.

- BRAIN Initiative (NIH): $600M+ invested; 2025 vision emphasizes multi-scale imaging and AI integration for dynamic brain models.

- Private Funding: Billionaires (e.g., via Neuralink's Elon Musk) fund BCIs; Foresight Institute workshops highlight WBE for AI safety (human-aligned via brain copies).

- Academic/Industry: EPFL's Blue Brain; Meta's AI decoders; Neurable's EEG headphones for focus tracking.

Philosophical, Ethical, and Societal Implications

- Identity and Consciousness: Debates rage—e.g., does uploading create a copy or transfer "you"? 2025 Journal of Consciousness Studies argues for "selective optimism," possible for cognition but not qualia (subjective experience).

- Ethics: Ownership of digital minds? Inequality in access? Risks of "digital gods" (evolved UIs) or corporate control. Neurorights violations (e.g., non-consensual modulation) are concerns, especially with "Hive Mind" speculations.

- Society: Potential for digital immortality, but disruptions in labor (AI-merged minds) and privacy. Shows like Pantheon (Netflix, 2025 buzz) explore these via uploaded consciousness narratives.

Future Outlook

While 2025 marks BCI maturation (e.g., commercial implants), full mind uploading hinges on resolving consciousness puzzles and scaling compute/scan tech. Projections: Mouse-brain emulation by 2030; human by 2045–2100. Progress is accelerating with AI (e.g., GPT-style models for decoding), but ethical guardrails are crucial.

APPENDIX

Fallow Lands And Bumper Crops

In agricultural science, bumper crops—exceptionally large harvests—are often associated with improved soil conditions, which can be influenced by leaving land fallow. Leaving land fallow means allowing it to rest without planting crops for a period, typically a season or a year, to restore soil fertility, structure, and organic matter. The relationship between fallowing and bumper crops depends on several factors, including soil type, climate, crop rotation practices, and the duration of the fallow period. Here's a detailed explanation:

Soil Fertility Restoration: When land is left fallow, it has time to recover nutrients depleted by previous crops. Natural processes like decomposition of organic matter, nitrogen fixation (especially if cover crops or legumes are used during the fallow period), and microbial activity replenish soil nutrients. This can lead to bumper crops in the season immediately following the fallow period, as crops benefit from the revitalized soil.

Timing of Bumper Crops: Bumper crops are most likely to occur in the first or second growing season after a fallow period, assuming other conditions (weather, pest control, etc.) are favorable. The exact timing depends on the fallowing method:

Traditional Fallowing: Land is left unplanted for a full season or year. Crops planted in the subsequent season often yield higher due to improved soil health.

Green Fallowing: Cover crops (e.g., clover or vetch) are grown during the fallow period to enrich the soil. When these are plowed under, the next crop planted—typically within the same or next growing season—can produce a bumper harvest due to enhanced soil fertility and structure.

Short-Term Fallowing: In some systems, fields are left fallow for only part of a season. The subsequent crop may still benefit, but the effect might be less pronounced than with longer fallow periods.

Crop Rotation Context: Fallowing is often part of a crop rotation system. For example, a field might be fallow one year, followed by a nutrient-demanding crop like corn or wheat the next year. These crops can produce bumper yields due to the nutrient buildup during the fallow period. The likelihood of a bumper crop diminishes in subsequent years if intensive farming resumes without further soil management.

Other Factors Influencing Bumper Crops:

Climate and Rainfall: Even with fallowing, bumper crops depend on favorable weather. For instance, fallowing in dry regions can conserve soil moisture, leading to better yields in the next season if rainfall is adequate.

Soil Type: Sandy soils may benefit less from fallowing than loamy or clay-rich soils, which retain nutrients better.

Management Practices: Incorporating organic matter or using cover crops during fallowing can amplify the potential for bumper crops compared to bare fallowing.

Historical and Modern Context: In traditional agriculture, such as medieval three-field systems, fields were left fallow every third year, and the crops planted in the following year often yielded significantly more. Modern agriculture may use shorter fallow periods or "active" fallowing with cover crops, leading to bumper crops in the next planting cycle, often within 6–12 months after fallowing.

Summary: Bumper crops are most expected in the first growing season after a fallow period, typically within 6–12 months, when soil fertility, structure, and moisture are optimized. The exact timing and yield depend on the fallowing method, crop type, and environmental conditions. For precise predictions, local agricultural data and practices would need to be considered.

APPENDIX

Skills That Humans Lack At Birth, That Other Animals Have

Humans are born with fewer innate skills compared to many animals, a trait tied to our species' prolonged development and reliance on learning. This is due to humans being altricial (born relatively helpless) rather than precocial (born more developed and independent), like many animals. Below is a concise overview of skills that many animals possess at birth but humans lack, grounded in biological and evolutionary perspectives, with examples for clarity.

1. Locomotion and Mobility

- Animal Abilities: Many animals can move independently shortly after birth, enabling them to evade predators or follow their group.

    - Examples:

        - Ungulates like antelopes or horses stand and walk within hours (e.g., a wildebeest calf runs within minutes to escape predators).

        - Sea turtles crawl to the ocean immediately after hatching.

        - Chickens and other precocial birds walk and peck for food soon after hatching.

Humans: Newborns lack the muscle strength, coordination, and neural development for walking or crawling. Humans typically begin crawling around 6-12 months and walking around 1 year, requiring extensive brain and muscle maturation.

2. Sensory-Motor Coordination

- Animal Abilities: Many animals exhibit precise sensory-motor skills at birth, allowing them to interact with their environment effectively.

  - Examples:

    - Ducklings imprint on and follow their mother within hours, using visual and auditory cues (imprinting studied by Konrad Lorenz).

    - Newborn dolphins swim alongside their mothers, coordinating with her movements using echolocation rudiments.

    - Spiders spin webs instinctively soon after hatching, relying on innate neural patterns.

- Humans: Human newborns have basic reflexes (e.g., grasping, sucking), but lack fine motor skills or purposeful sensory-motor integration. Hand-eye coordination develops gradually over months, with purposeful grasping emerging around 3-6 months.

3. Survival Instincts and Foraging

- Animal Abilities: Many animals are born with instincts to find food or evade danger without parental instruction.

  - Examples:

    - Newborn sharks swim away and hunt independently, relying on innate predatory instincts.

- Kangaroo joeys instinctively crawl to their mother's pouch to nurse after birth.

- Many fish, like salmon fry, begin feeding on microorganisms shortly after hatching.

- Humans: Human infants are entirely dependent on caregivers for food and safety. They lack foraging skills or the ability to seek sustenance beyond the rooting reflex for nursing, with self-feeding not developing until around 6-12 months (and even then, requiring assistance).

4. Communication and Social Interaction

- Animal Abilities: Some animals are born with innate communication abilities to signal needs or bond with their group.

  - Examples:

  - Chicks cheep to communicate distress or hunger immediately after hatching.

  - Elephant calves vocalize and integrate into herd dynamics within days, using low-frequency rumbles.

  - Wolf pups whimper or howl rudimentarily to signal needs soon after birth.

- Humans: Newborns cry as a basic distress signal but lack specific vocal communication skills. Language development begins with babbling around 6 months, maturing much later (2-3 years for basic speech), heavily reliant on social learning rather than instinct.

5. Thermoregulation and Environmental Adaptation

- Animal Abilities: Many animals can regulate body temperature or adapt to their environment shortly after birth.

  - Examples:

    - Arctic fox pups, born with fur, begin thermoregulating within days, aided by innate burrowing behaviors.

    - Crocodile hatchlings regulate body temperature by moving between sun and shade instinctively.

    - Penguin chicks maintain warmth with downy feathers and huddling behavior soon after hatching.

- Humans: Human newborns cannot regulate body temperature effectively, relying on external warmth (e.g., swaddling, caregiver contact). Thermoregulation matures over weeks, with no innate environmental adaptation skills at birth.

6. Predator Avoidance and Defensive Behaviors

- Animal Abilities: Many animals are born with instincts to hide, flee, or defend against threats.

  - Examples:

    - Fawns freeze or lie still to avoid detection by predators, an innate camouflage response.

    - Baby snakes (e.g., rattlesnakes) can deliver venomous bites shortly after birth.

- Octopus hatchlings release ink clouds to escape predators instinctively.

- Humans: Newborns lack any defensive capabilities beyond crying to alert caregivers. They are entirely dependent on adults for protection, with no innate predator-avoidance behaviors.

Why the Difference?

- Evolutionary Trade-Offs: Humans' large brains (relative to body size) require birth before full neurological and physical development to fit through the pelvis, leading to prolonged dependency. This altricial nature allows for extensive learning, cultural transmission, and cognitive flexibility, which are human strengths but absent at birth.

- Animal Precociality: Precocial animals (e.g., horses, ducks) prioritize immediate survival in predator-heavy environments, sacrificing cognitive plasticity for hardwired instincts. Even semi-altricial animals (e.g., primates) often have more innate skills than humans at birth.

- Brain Development: Human brains are ~25% of adult size at birth, compared to ~50-70% in precocial animals like calves or foals. This necessitates a longer post-birth period for neural wiring, delaying skill acquisition.

Jewish Scriptural Context

While not directly addressing animal skills, Jewish scriptures emphasize humanity's unique role in creation (Genesis 1:26-28, dominion over animals) and dependence on divine sustenance (Psalms 104:29-30, God's continuous creation).

Texts like Midrash Rabbah (8:1) suggest creation serves humanity's spiritual purpose, implying that humans' lack of innate skills at birth is offset by their capacity for moral and intellectual growth, aligning with the idea that the universe is sustained for human potential (as discussed earlier).

Summary
Humans lack innate skills like locomotion (walking/running), sensory-motor coordination (e.g., web-spinning), foraging, communication (beyond crying), thermoregulation, and predator avoidance, which many animals—especially precocial species like ungulates, birds, or reptiles—possess at birth. This stems from humans' altricial nature, prioritizing brain development and learning over immediate independence.

APPENDIX

Merging Of Souls And Minds

Several philosophical, spiritual, and scientific theories explore the idea of souls or minds merging into a collective or unified state. Below are the key theories and concepts that align with this idea:

1. Collective Consciousness (Jungian Psychology):

- Overview: Carl Jung proposed the concept of the collective unconscious, a shared reservoir of archetypes and experiences that connects all human minds. While not a literal merging of souls, it suggests a deep interconnection of individual psyches.

- Key Idea: Individual minds tap into a shared layer of consciousness, influencing thoughts, dreams, and behaviors across humanity.

- Source: Jung's Psychological Types and Archetypes and the Collective Unconscious.

2. Panpsychism:

- Overview: Panpsychism posits that consciousness is a fundamental property of the universe, present in all matter to varying degrees. Some interpretations suggest that individual minds or consciousnesses could merge into a universal consciousness.

- Key Idea: All minds are interconnected as part of a cosmic consciousness, potentially unifying at a fundamental level.

- Source: Philosophers like David Chalmers and Philip Goff.

3. Omega Point (Teilhard de Chardin) [Referenced in *The Fusion Threshold*]:

- **Overview: Pierre Teilhard de Chardin, a Jesuit priest and philosopher, proposed the Omega Point, a future state where all consciousness converges into a single, unified divine consciousness. This is driven by the evolution of complexity and consciousness.**

- **Key Idea: Human minds and souls evolve toward a collective unity with God or a cosmic consciousness.**

- **Source: Teilhard's The Phenomenon of Man.**

4. Buddhist Concepts of Interconnectedness:

- Overview: In Buddhism, particularly in Mahayana traditions, the concept of interdependence (Pratityasamutpada) and the non-self (Anatta) suggest that individual souls or minds are not separate but part of an interconnected web. Enlightenment involves dissolving the illusion of a separate self, merging into a universal awareness.

- Key Idea: The individual mind merges with the ultimate reality (Nirvana) or universal consciousness.

- Source: Buddhist texts like the Heart Sutra and teachings of Thich Nhat Hanh.

5. Transhumanist Singularity:

- **Overview: Some transhumanist theories, particularly those related to the technological singularity, propose that advanced technology (e.g., brain-computer interfaces) could lead to a merging of human minds into a collective digital consciousness.**

- **Key Idea: Individual minds could upload and integrate into a shared digital or cosmic intelligence.**

- **Source: Works by Ray Kurzweil, such as The Singularity Is Near.**

Mystical Traditions (e.g., Sufism, Kabbalah):

- Overview: In mystical traditions like Sufism (Islam) and Kabbalah (Judaism), the soul's journey involves reuniting with the divine source. This can be seen as a merging of individual souls into a unified divine essence.

- Key Idea: The soul dissolves into the divine unity, losing its individuality in God.

- Source: Writings of Rumi (Sufism) and the Zohar (Kabbalah).

APPENDIX

Basic Physical Constants And "Goldilocks Zones"

The idea that basic physical constants lie within "Goldilocks Zones" refers to the fine-tuning argument in cosmology, which suggests that certain fundamental physical constants have values that fall within a narrow range, enabling the existence of life as we know it. These constants govern the fundamental forces and properties of the universe, and even slight deviations from their observed values could render the universe inhospitable to life.

What Are Physical Constants and the Goldilocks Zone?

Physical constants are universal values that govern the behavior of physical systems, such as the speed of light, the gravitational constant, or the strength of fundamental forces. The "Goldilocks Zone" in this context means that these constants have values that are "just right" for the formation of stable galaxies, stars, planets, and ultimately life. If these constants were slightly different, the universe might be too chaotic, too uniform, or otherwise incapable of supporting complex structures or life.

The fine-tuning argument posits that the precise values of these constants are unlikely to occur by chance, as the range of life-permitting values is extremely narrow compared to the theoretically possible range.

Examples of Physical Constants in Goldilocks Zones

Here are some key physical constants and how their values appear finely tuned for a life-permitting universe:

- Gravitational Constant (G):

• Role: Determines the strength of gravity, which governs the formation of stars, galaxies, and planets.

• Goldilocks Zone: If G were slightly stronger, stars would collapse too quickly, burning out before life could evolve. If weaker, stars and planets wouldn't form, as matter wouldn't clump together effectively. For example, physicist Brandon Carter estimated that a change in G by more than a factor of ~2 could prevent star formation or make stars burn too rapidly.

2. Electromagnetic Fine-Structure Constant ($\alpha \approx 1/137$):

• Role: Governs the strength of the electromagnetic force, which holds atoms together and drives chemical reactions essential for life.

• Goldilocks Zone: If α were slightly larger (e.g., >0.1), atoms would become unstable, and fusion in stars would be disrupted. If smaller (e.g., <0.005), chemical bonding would be too weak to form complex molecules. The observed value allows stable atoms and molecules like DNA.

3. Strong Nuclear Force Constant:

• Role: Determines the strength of the force that binds protons and neutrons in atomic nuclei.

• Goldilocks Zone: A ~2% increase would prevent proton formation in the early universe, leaving no atoms. A ~2% decrease would make nuclei unstable, preventing the formation of heavy

elements like carbon and oxygen, which are
essential for life.

4. Cosmological Constant (Λ):

- Role: Governs the rate of the universe's
expansion, driven by dark energy.

- Goldilocks Zone: The observed value is
incredibly small ($\sim 10^{-122}$ in Planck units). If Λ
were slightly larger, the universe would expand
too rapidly for galaxies to form. If negative or
too small, the universe could collapse before life
emerges. The viable range is estimated to be within
1 part in 10^{120} of its observed value.

5. Ratio of Electromagnetic to Gravitational Forces ($N \approx 10^{36}$):

- Role: Sets the relative strength of
electromagnetic and gravitational forces between
particles like protons.

- Goldilocks Zone: If this ratio were much
smaller, stars would be too small and short-lived
to support planetary systems. If much larger, stars
would be too massive and unstable. The balance
allows for stable, long-lived stars like our Sun.

6. Mass Ratio of Fundamental Particles (e.g., Electron to
Proton Mass):

- Role: Affects the stability of atoms and the
chemistry of life.

- Goldilocks Zone: The electron's mass is

about 1/1836 that of the proton. A significant change could disrupt atomic stability or prevent the formation of stable chemical bonds, making complex chemistry impossible.

Why Are These Considered "Goldilocks Zones"?

The term "Goldilocks Zone" is borrowed from the concept of planetary habitability, where conditions are "just right" for liquid water. For physical constants, the analogy holds because:

- Narrow Range: Calculations show that life-permitting values occupy a tiny fraction of the possible range. For example, physicist Roger Penrose noted that the entropy of the early universe (related to cosmological parameters) is fine-tuned to 1 part in $10^{10^{123}}$, an almost unimaginable precision.

- Sensitivity to Change: Small deviations in these constants lead to catastrophic outcomes, like a universe with no stars, no atoms, or no stable chemistry. For instance, a 1% change in the strong force could prevent carbon-based life.

- Interdependence: Many constants are interconnected, so altering one (e.g., the strong force) affects others (e.g., nuclear fusion rates), amplifying the need for precise balance.

Explanations for Fine-Tuning. The fine-tuning of physical constants has sparked debate, with several proposed explanations:

1. Anthropic Principle: We observe these constants because only a life-permitting universe allows observers to

exist. This is often tied to the multiverse hypothesis, where many universes exist with different constants, and we happen to be in one that supports life.

2. Design Hypothesis: Some argue that the precise values suggest a purposeful intelligent design, though this is a philosophical rather than scientific claim.

3. Undiscovered Physics: The constants might be determined by a deeper, yet-undiscovered theory (e.g., string theory), where their values are not arbitrary but fixed by fundamental principles.

4. Chance: The constants could simply be a lucky coincidence, though the extreme improbability makes this less satisfying to some.

Challenges and Context

- Theoretical Ranges: The "possible" range of constants is often based on theoretical assumptions, as we don't fully know the constraints on these values in a complete theory of physics.

- Life's Definition: The fine-tuning argument often assumes carbon-based life as the standard. Other forms of life might be possible under different conditions, though this is speculative.

- Scientific Limits: While the fine-tuning is well-documented, explanations like the multiverse or design remain speculative, as they are difficult to test empirically.

Conclusion

The basic physical constants, such as the gravitational constant, electromagnetic fine-structure constant, and cosmological constant, appear to lie within extraordinarily narrow "Goldilocks Zones" that allow for a universe capable of supporting stars, planets, and life. Small changes in these values could lead to a universe without atoms, stars, or chemistry, making the observed values seem remarkably precise. While this fine-tuning is a fascinating feature of our universe, its ultimate explanation—whether due to a multiverse, deeper physics, or another mechanism—remains an open question in cosmology.

APPENDIX

Higher Dimensions And Noah's Ark And The Ark Of The Covenant

Ark of the Covenant
The Ark of the Covenant, described in Exodus as a gold-covered acacia wood chest measuring 2.5 cubits long by 1.5 cubits wide and high, exhibited phenomena interpreted as ties to higher spatial dimensions. Talmudic tradition states that the Ark occupied no physical space in the Holy of Holies despite its size, creating a paradoxical overlap where measurements from its sides to the room's walls equaled the full expected distance on both sides—suggesting a non-Euclidean geometry or intrusion from a fourth dimension.

Its placement within the cubic Holy of Holies evokes a tesseract (4D hypercube), with the Ark as a 3D projection enclosing higher-dimensional space, and biblical references to God's multidimensional love (width, length, height, depth) reinforce this as a portal-like interface between realms.

Anomalous events, like plagues on captors and the Shechinah glory's descent, imply extradimensional energy manifestations.

Noah's Ark
Noah's Ark, built to Genesis-specified dimensions of 300 cubits long, 50 wide, and 30 high, shows subtler links to higher dimensions through its tri-level structure mirroring layers of reality: physical (lower deck), informational/mathematical (middle), and spiritual (upper), as a microcosm transcending 3D constraints to preserve life across existential planes.

While lacking direct spatial anomalies, biblical flood survival and post-flood repopulation imply improbable containment and preservation, potentially enabled by higher-dimensional folding of space or time—echoing broader scriptural motifs of disappearances into extra dimensions.

Modern searches highlight geological anomalies like boat-shaped formations, but these are earthly rather than extradimensional.

Moshiach's Tasks

The concept of the Moshiach (Messiah) in Jewish tradition involves a figure who will fulfill specific tasks to usher in a redemptive era. Based on traditional sources, primarily drawn from the Torah, Talmud, and later Jewish thought, the Moshiach is expected to accomplish the following:

1. Restoration of the Davidic Monarchy: The Moshiach, a human leader from the Davidic line, will reestablish the Davidic dynasty, ruling as a righteous king over Israel.

2. Ingathering of the Exiles: He will gather all Jews back to the Land of Israel, ending the diaspora and restoring the nation to its ancestral homeland.

3. Rebuilding the Temple: The Moshiach will oversee the construction of the Third Temple in Jerusalem, restoring the central place of Jewish worship.

4. Restoration of Torah Observance: He will reinstitute full adherence to Torah law, including the reinvigoration of the Sanhedrin and the sacrificial system, fostering universal Torah study and practice.

5. Universal Peace: The Moshiach will bring about an era of global peace, where "nation shall not lift up sword against nation" (Isaiah 2:4), **resolving conflicts and establishing harmony.**

6. **Universal Knowledge of God: He will lead humanity to recognize and worship the one God, spreading monotheistic faith and moral clarity worldwide, as prophesied in Zechariah 14:9.**

7. Redemption and Spiritual Renewal: The Messianic era will bring spiritual and physical redemption, including the resurrection of the dead and the **elimination of evil**, disease, and suffering.

www.ingramcontent.com/pod-product-compliance
Lightning Source LLC
Chambersburg PA
CBHW072241270326
41930CB00010B/2223